Advanced Introduction to US Civil Liberties

Elgar Advanced Introductions are stimulating and thoughtful introductions to major fields in the social sciences, business and law, expertly written by the world's leading scholars. Designed to be accessible yet rigorous, they offer concise and lucid surveys of the substantive and policy issues associated with discrete subject areas.

The aims of the series are two-fold: to pinpoint essential principles of a particular field, and to offer insights that stimulate critical thinking. By distilling the vast and often technical corpus of information on the subject into a concise and meaningful form, the books serve as accessible introductions for undergraduate and graduate students coming to the subject for the first time. Importantly, they also develop well-informed, nuanced critiques of the field that will challenge and extend the understanding of advanced students, scholars and policy-makers.

For a full list of titles in the series please see the back of the book. Recent titles in the series include:

Water Economics and Policy
Ariel Dinar

Disaster Risk Reduction
Douglas Paton

Social Movements and Political Protests
Karl-Dieter Opp

Radical Innovation
Joe Tidd

Pricing Strategy and Analytics
Vithala R. Rao

Bounded Rationality
Clement A. Tisdell

International Food Law
Neal D. Fortin

International Conflict and Security Law
Second Edition
Nigel D. White

Entrepreneurial Finance
Second Edition
Hans Landström

US Civil Liberties
Susan N. Herman

Advanced Introduction to

US Civil Liberties

SUSAN N. HERMAN

*Ruth Bader Ginsburg Professor of Law, Brooklyn Law
School; President Emeritus, American Civil Liberties Union,
USA*

Elgar Advanced Introductions

 **Edward Elgar**
PUBLISHING

Cheltenham, UK • Northampton, MA, USA

Published by
Edward Elgar Publishing Limited
The Lypiatts
15 Lansdown Road
Cheltenham
Glos GL50 2JA
UK

Edward Elgar Publishing, Inc.
William Pratt House
9 Dewey Court
Northampton
Massachusetts 01060
USA

A catalogue record for this book
is available from the British Library

Library of Congress Control Number: 2023931303

This book is available electronically on Elgar Advanced Introductions: Law
(www.advancedintros.com)

Printed on elemental chlorine free (ECF)
recycled paper containing 30% Post-Consumer Waste

ISBN 978 1 80037 665 6 (cased)
ISBN 978 1 80037 667 0 (paperback)
ISBN 978 1 80037 666 3 (eBook)

Printed and bound in the USA

This book is dedicated to the board and staff members of the ACLU and its affiliates, past, present, and future, for their tireless work in growing and defending US civil liberties.

Contents

Introduction to US civil liberties

As Roger Baldwin, founding director of the American Civil Liberties Union, frequently remarked, 'No battle for civil liberties ever remains won.'

US history has been marked by pendulum swings in the level of realization of virtually every civil liberty.

As this book will describe, the twentieth century saw dramatic growth in the protection of rights, from the freedom of speech and assembly to due process, to reproductive freedom, peaking in the 1960s and 1970s. Twenty-first century law – in state legislatures as well as the US Supreme Court – has been reversing course in many areas, sometimes incrementally and sometimes abruptly. During the 1960s, for example, the Warren Court[1] issued landmark decisions checking state attempts to discourage or discount the votes of Black citizens; the twenty-first century Supreme Court has allowed states to adopt hundreds of regressive voting laws and procedures and has itself gutted ameliorative federal voting rights legislation (see Chapter 12). In 1973, the US Supreme Court declared that the Constitution guarantees a fundamental right to choose to have an abortion; in 2022, the Court summarily reversed that decision, leaving the states free to pass laws criminalizing or sharply limiting the availability of abortion in about half the country (see Section 10.4). States discouraging demonstrations, banning classroom discussions of controversial issues like race and sexual orientation, and allocating tax dollars to religious schools increasingly threaten hard won rights that had seemed established.

---

[1] Earl Warren was Chief Justice from 1953 to 1969. In his first term, he mustered a unanimous Court to declare racial segregation in schools unconstitutional, foreshadowing many other landmark Warren Court decisions favoring due process and equality.

Volatility is inevitable because the United States is deeply divided in its attitudes and expectations. Although Americans might generally profess belief in common core civil liberties principles – like freedom of speech and religion and due process – they have very different ideas about what those liberties should mean in practice. Does 'freedom of speech' mean that one has a right to make racist statements, to burn a flag, or to spend unlimited amounts in a political campaign? Does freedom of religion mean that prayer should be allowed in public schools? Do due process norms allow suspected terrorists to be detained without a hearing?

The different answers Americans would give to these questions are rooted in their various views of the nature of the US Constitution, their prioritization of values, their individual risk assessment, and more generally in their politics. The variables briefly summarized here are themes that will recur throughout the book.

The Function of Constitutional Rights. The American public as well as judges maintain very different understandings of the purpose and function of the rights enshrined in the US Constitution, the chief source in the United States for protection of civil liberties. Some perceive the Constitution as quintessentially and broadly libertarian. In many traditional accounts, the central justification for constitutional civil liberties is said to be the prevention of tyranny. Libertarians tend to view a large swath of government regulation as tyrannical and thus may contend that the Constitution should be understood to prohibit many kinds of governmental interference with individual choice – not only choice of the explicitly covered freedom of religion and speech, but perhaps also decisions like entering into an employment contract or refusing a vaccination. With the assistance of the courts, rights can give the individual a veto over repressive laws abridging unpopular expression (like racist speech or burning a flag) or religious observances, or over the progressive policy decisions embodied in labor, health, environmental, and civil rights laws.

To non-libertarians – people who are more inclined to believe that government may and should act to serve the public interest – there may seem to be less need for the restraints imposed by rights. Non-libertarians may place a higher value on respecting the policy decisions made by elected government officials and therefore argue that the courts should be hesitant to override those choices by defining rights broadly. The courts should not, for example, infer a constitutional right to freedom of contract that disarms labor laws, or an individual right to refuse to get a vaccination that could compromise public health. Courts might also choose narrower definitions of explicit constitutional rights. If the First Amendment were viewed as only providing special protection for political and other highly valued forms of speech, for example, government would then be free to regulate other forms of expression like obscenity or commercial advertising.

Judges and scholars generally agree that the Constitution confers some rights that are intended to be counter-majoritarian, but diverge on the question of what those rights are. Some Supreme Court Justices count the right to abortion, like freedom of speech, as a fundamental right not subject to legislative discretion and regard gun control as a proper subject for legislative policymaking. Other Justices regard abortion as unprotected by the US Constitution and the right to bear arms as an important counter-majoritarian check on overbearing gun control laws.

Another critique of libertarian civil liberties jurisprudence springs from egalitarian principles. The eighteenth-century Constitution that libertarians cherish was written by elite white men and ratified by only a fraction of the people of the United States. Women, people of color, and men without property could not vote and so were not included in the original Constitution's definition of 'We, the people.' The Constitution exalted liberty but did not even mention equality. Egalitarian critics advocate greater attention to the more inclusive values of the Constitution as amended after the Civil War rather than reverence for the world view of the Constitution's original authors and ratifiers.

Because racial and other minorities often have reason to be skeptical about deferring to political majorities, egalitarians may look to the Constitution – both the Bill of Rights and the Reconstruction Amendments – to check laws that have a disproportionate impact on minorities. The Fourth Amendment protection against unreasonable searches and seizures, for example, might heed the perspective of Black and Brown people who suffer from broad police discretion that a majority of Americans might find unobjectionable (see Section 8.5). The First Amendment freedom of expression might be interpreted as aimed at ensuring that everyone is fully included in democratic dialogue, perhaps providing a theoretical basis for arguing that laws limiting campaign expenditures are not inconsistent with the Constitution (see Section 5.6). The Fourteenth Amendment might even be viewed as providing a basis for deriving affirmative governmental obligations to reduce the consequences of economic inequality (see Section 1.4).

Visions of the Constitution tend to correlate with partisan politics, with Republicans generally favoring a more libertarian and less egalitarian orientation.

Methods of Constitutional Interpretation. The greatest schism in theories about how best to interpret the Constitution is between those who contend that the meaning of the Constitution is fixed by history, and those who believe that constitutional protections should evolve to address contemporary threats to liberty and contemporary mores. Although sometimes identifying different sources as dispositive, originalist judges and scholars argue that the Constitution should be interpreted to mean what its authors and ratifiers – of the Bill of Rights in the eighteenth century and of the Reconstruction Amendments in the nineteenth century – would have understood its words to mean. Textualists disavow any interest in direct evidence of the framers' intent, but strictly construe the words of the Constitution as freezing its meaning in time. Thus a history-oriented Supreme Court once held that wiretapping a telephone was not a 'search' or 'seizure' within the meaning of the Fourth Amendment and so was not subject to any constitutional limitation because the eighteenth-century understanding of those words would only have included physical intrusions.[2] In deciding that the Second Amendment guarantees individuals a right to bear arms not contingent on serving in a militia,[3] the twenty-first century Court relied heavily on eighteenth-century dictionaries.

The opposing view is that the Constitution, written in very general language, was intended to evolve and to accommodate later developments – such as developing technologies that give the government new methods

---

[2]   Olmstead v. United States, 277 U.S. 438 (1928). See Section 8.3 for discussion.

[3]   District of Columbia v. Heller, 554 U.S. 570 (2008). The Second Amendment enigmatically provides: 'A well regulated Militia, being necessary to the security of a free State, the right of the people to keep and bear Arms, shall not be infringed.'

of spying on people, or evolving standards of tolerance.[4] The Constitution prohibits 'cruel and unusual punishment' rather than listing particular forms of punishment the framers disapproved. As Justice Anthony Kennedy said in a case finding a Texas law criminalizing consensual sodomy to be unconstitutional,

> Had those who drew and ratified the Due Process Clauses of the Fifth Amendment or the Fourteenth Amendment known the components of liberty in its manifold possibilities, they might have been more specific. They did not presume to have this insight. They knew times can blind us to certain truths and later generations can see that laws once thought necessary and proper in fact serve only to oppress. As the Constitution endures, persons in every generation can invoke its principles in their own search for greater freedom.[5]

In this view, the framers' and ratifiers' understanding and goals are still considered relevant, but at a different level of generality. The authors of the Fourth Amendment are viewed as aiming to protect a right to be let alone against unjustifiable intrusion of any type, not just physical invasions.

Originalists object that the Constitution should only be updated through the cumbersome amendment process because judges expounding the Constitution will subjectively impose their own political preferences. Non-originalists respond that originalists impose *their* own political preferences by their choice of a backward-looking approach to interpretation and that, in any event, history is not an objective referent. Originalist judges are necessarily selective in their sources, even including their choice of dictionaries.

Balancing Rights and Public Interests. Even where everyone would agree that a constitutional right exists, no right is absolute. As Justice Oliver Wendell Holmes famously observed, 'the most stringent protection of free speech would not protect a man in falsely shouting fire in a theater and causing panic.'[6] Freedom of religion would not guarantee a right to human sacrifice. But under what circumstances should the public interest be considered to outweigh an individual right and how is a proper balance

---

[4]   Ronald Dworkin, *Taking Rights Seriously* (Cambridge, MA: Harvard University Press, 1977).

[5]   Lawrence v. Texas, 539 U.S. 558 (2003).

[6]   Schenck v. United States, 249 U.S. 47 (1919), 25–6; see also Section 3.3.

to be struck? People will be more willing to minimize or make exceptions to individual liberty interests if they believe that generous protection of a liberty will compromise competing goals like safety, school discipline, crime control, or national security.

American history has been a perpetual contest between the assertion that the Constitution is 'not a suicide pact'[7] – and thus it is sometimes necessary to give up some degree of civil liberty in service of other goals – and Benjamin Franklin's warning that 'Those who would give up essential Liberty, to purchase a little temporary Safety, deserve neither Liberty nor Safety.'[8] People inevitably will differ in their assessments of the essentiality of a right – should due process protections in criminal proceedings be expansive because it is better, as William Blackstone said, to let ten guilty people go free rather than convict one innocent?[9] And they will differ in their assessments of how much risk they might have to tolerate if rights are prioritized. Does providing robust due process protections for people accused of crime put the public at significantly greater risk of being victimized? Risk assessment, especially in times of war or perceived emergency, may be more emotional than rational. Do laws repressing speech or permitting broad surveillance actually help to win wars and guarantee safety? Might some harsh anti-terrorism measures be not only ineffective but counterproductive?

Hierarchy of Values; Liberty and Equality. Disagreement also arises about how to mediate among multiple values or rights when they conflict. A classic example occurs when freedom of the press to report on a criminal trial interferes with the fairness of that trial.

One important contemporary question is how to reconcile the demands of rights and equality. Is equality a value that is consistent with and complements claims of liberty, or does it challenge and potentially undermine civil liberties? For one example of this debate, see Section 5.3 on First Amendment protection for hate speech. The value of equality also com-

---

7   Terminiello v. Chicago (1949) (Jackson, J., dissenting): 'An old proverb warns us to take heed lest we "walk into a well from looking at the stars".

8   Pennsylvania Assembly: Reply to the Governor November 11, 1755, Founders Online, National Archives, https://founders.archives.gov/documents/Franklin/01-06-02-0107.

9   William Blackstone, *Commentaries on the Laws of England* (Oxford: Clarendon Press, 1765–1770).

plicates what is traditionally characterized as a zero-sum balance between claims of liberty and public safety in the context of search and seizure, criminal law, and anti-terrorism efforts (see Section 8.5). It is one thing to be willing to give up one's own liberty in pursuit of safety; it is quite another to adopt security measures likely to sacrifice only the liberty of Muslims.

Lessons from History. Occasions when the government overreacted to per-ceived threats and trampled civil liberties in the name of safety– like the 1798 Alien and Sedition Acts or the xenophobia and repression of speech during and following World War I – have left scars on the American psyche. Chapter 3 provides some prominent examples. Arguments about current civil liberties controversies often center on comparison with past embarrassments, a form of negative history: what should not be done again. When President Donald Trump issued his Executive Order imposing strict immigration controls mostly on Muslims, for example, one central point of contention was whether this discrimination was com-parable to the racist treatment of loyal Japanese Americans during World War II (see Section 3.4). Judicial opinions that history has deemed wrong-headed can become tropes. Dissenting Justices who want to forcefully depict a majority opinion as dangerous judicial overreaching invoke the infamous *Dred Scott*[10] case, where the Supreme Court's declaration that the Due Process Clause prevented Congress from depriving slaveholders of their "property" contributed to the inevitability of the Civil War.

Decision-makers. The most important variable determining how much protection civil liberties will enjoy is the identity of the judges and elected officials in a position to either enforce or minimize civil liberties. The US Supreme Court has played a special role as final arbiter of the meaning of rights. This is because of the American version of the doctrine of judicial review, traced back to the foundational 1803 case of *Marbury v. Madison.*[11] Changes in the composition of the Court can lead to dramatic changes in civil liberties law across the country. But the Supreme Court is not the only entity with power over civil liberties. Chapter 4 discusses the role of Congress, the federal executive branch, and the states, all of whom

---

[10]   Dred Scott v. Sandford, 60 U.S. 393 (1857), found that slaveholders had a constitutional right to possess their 'property' and enslaved people did not even have the right to bring a lawsuit.

[11]   5 U.S. 137 (1803).

are bound by oath to support the US Constitution, and all of whom can increase civil liberties protections above the federal constitutional floor or can cynically hollow out declared rights.

Americans like to believe that the United States is exceptional in its robust protection of civil liberties. But as recent Supreme Court decisions have shown, those protections rise and fall. Ever since the growth of judicial review of First Amendment claims in the twentieth century, the Supreme Court has provided strong protection for the rights a majority of Justices favor. The twenty-first century Roberts Court favors robust protection of free speech in a libertarian vein, and has been enhancing the level of protection for individual freedom of religion at the expense of protection against establishment of religion (see Chapter 7). In 2008, the Roberts Court reversed previous interpretations of the Second Amendment and declared the existence of an individual right to bear arms, giving the Court a veto over state and federal gun control laws. At a time when dozens of countries were adopting protections of the right to choose to have an abortion, the Court rescinded federal norms that had prevailed for almost half a century. And except during the brief era of the Warren Court, the Supreme Court has failed miserably at valuing or promoting equality. While the Justices claim not to be politically motivated, their positions do tend to map onto the partisan views of the presidents who appointed them, currently a solid Republican majority.

The Democracy Index now ranks the United States as a flawed rather than a full democracy. Compared with hybrid and authoritarian regimes, the United States does enjoy strong protection for due process rights and many liberties. But some of the recent civil liberties choices of the Supreme Court and state legislatures threaten democracy, moving the country closer to authoritarianism, and are undemocratic in the sense that they do not represent the values of most Americans. A supermajority of the American people supports the right to choose to have an abortion, for example, and supports gun control laws. But the policy choices of a minority of Americans, as in the recent abortion and gun control cases, have become dominant in the Supreme Court and also in state and federal legislatures due to a combination of structural features built into the US Constitution and condonation of voter suppression laws and partisan gerrymandering (see Chapter 12).

Public opinion polls also show Americans wavering on some protections of core civil liberties, including the pillars of democracy: freedom of speech, freedom of assembly, and freedom of the press. A growing number of Americans, on both sides of the political aisle, would be willing to make exceptions to the First Amendment to allow suppression of speech they hate rather than abide by the principle of content neutrality (see Section 5.3). Individuals and state governments show increasing intolerance of demonstrators or journalists expressing opinions they find disagreeable (see Sections 6.1 and 6.2). Most alarmingly, many people are willing to support non-neutral voting laws and practices they think will lead to their party's victory (see Chapter 12).

Is this a prologue to the future of US civil liberties, or will the pendulum continue to swing?

This book will begin in Part I with some definitions – what are 'civil liberties' as compared with human rights, civil rights, and constitutional rights? Chapters 2 and 3 will turn to history, sketching antecedents of the Constitution and some of the events leading to contemporary understandings of US civil liberties. Chapter 4 will address how civil liberties are implemented, by the courts, elected and appointed officials, and non-governmental organizations.

Part II will discuss some highlights of the history and content of protections for core constitutional civil liberties: freedom of speech, assembly, the press, and religion; search and seizure; family and reproductive freedom; due process in criminal cases. As the definitions in Section 1.1 show, this list could also include other rights. Equality and voting rights law will be covered in summary form in Chapters 11 and 12, not because these rights are not critically important but only for lack of space.

My perspective is informed by having taught Constitutional Law for over four decades and by my experience as President of the American Civil Liberties Union (ACLU), an organization that has played a major role in the history and development of US civil liberties. In writing this book, I am as committed to non-partisanship as I have always been in those roles. But the interplay of partisan politics and civil liberties cannot be ignored at a time when the two major political parties take diametrically opposed positions on most of the subjects discussed.

PART I

Background: perspectives on civil liberties

1   What are civil liberties?

1.1   Defining civil liberties

Distinguishing civil liberties, civil rights, human rights, and constitutional rights is not a simple task as there is considerable overlap among these categories and not everyone uses the terminology in the same manner.

The concept of 'civil liberty' defines liberal democracy, delimiting the relationship of the individual and the state. Authoritarian governments are characterized by a lack of civil liberty.

Civil liberties are prototypically understood as freedom *from* undue governmental interference. Government may not forbid people to criticize its actions, require people to follow a particular religion, or arbitrarily subject people to punishment. A typical list of core civil liberties would include freedom of speech/expression/conscience, religion, association, assembly, and the press; freedom from unreasonable searches and seizures; freedom regarding one's sexuality and family, including marriage, reproductive choice, and child-rearing; privacy; and due process, especially in criminal proceedings. To that list may be added the right to democratic participation – government cannot abridge the right to vote or to run for office – and to equal treatment under law.

In its list of the civil liberties constituting its mission, the ACLU includes many rights of equality as well as liberties: freedom from discrimination on the basis of race, gender, LGBTQ status, disability, and immigrants' rights. The breadth of this list rests on the perception that there is a critical nexus between liberty and equality, as well as among individual rights. During the 1960s, ACLU Board member Pauli Murray was one of the first to promote the concept of intersectionality: that the harm a person suffers may not fall neatly within a single category. Why, Murray asked, do we only talk about 'Jim Crow' and not 'Jane Crow,' the unique pattern of harms suffered by Black women?

1.2   Defining human rights

The precept that every person has innate human rights is based more on moral than political principles. Human rights are centered on the right of every person to self-realization more than on the need to constrain governmental actors. The Universal Declaration of Human Rights (UDHR), adopted by the United Nations in 1948, contains 30 articles which declare human rights to encompass a right to dignity and socioeconomic rights (like a right to housing) in addition to a wide range of civil liberties (like freedom of expression and freedom from arbitrary detention). The United Nations more generally defines the human rights it seeks to preserve as including 'the right to life and liberty, freedom from slavery and torture, freedom of opinion and expression, the right to work and education, and many more.'[1]

Although the United States signed the UDHR. it has not embraced human rights principles going beyond the narrower set of civil liberties enshrined in the US Constitution. The US conception of civil liberty was principally derived from English tradition, resulting in the adoption of chiefly negative rights – proscriptions as opposed to prescription for what government or individual people must or should do. European republican tradition offers a different touchstone: that the individual has an affirmative right to dignity and autonomy. Defining fundamental values as centered on innate individual human rights has many consequences, potentially obliging government to take action to preserve and promote those rights rather than simply refrain from particular intrusive actions. In this view, government is not just a potential threat to liberty but a potential solution to a wide range of problems. The South African Constitution, for example, provides a basis for affirmative socioeconomic rights including a right to have access to adequate housing, allowing courts to assess whether the government is fulfilling its responsibility.

---

[1]   See United Nations website: https://www.un.org/en/global-issues/human-rights.

Another facet of the pantheon of values in a human rights model is that individuals have a right to be treated equally, with no individual or group regarded as superior or inferior, and not to be used as a pawn in government actions. Human rights models may also provide norms for the conduct of private individuals, promoting everyone's dignity by expecting individuals to treat one another in a spirit of brotherhood. In France, fraternity is an equal part of a triumvirate of fundamental values along with liberty and equality.

1.3   Defining civil rights

Definitions of civil rights focus on the right to political and social freedom and equality. Unlike the US Constitution's version of civil liberties, a civil rights model would encompass affirmative rights applying not only to government but to private actors. Civil rights are more fully protected by legislation – federal and in some jurisdictions state or local – than by court-made law. The US Constitution almost never applies to private actors (see Section 4.3). The federal Civil Rights Act of 1964, Fair Housing Act, and Equal Pay Act all prohibit forms of private discrimination. While civil liberties limit governmental action, implementation of civil rights depends on action by governmental agencies, like the Equal Employment Opportunity Commission.

Any list of civil rights – the rights government should be obliged to protect – will substantially overlap with civil liberties. The US Commission on Civil Rights, for example, describes its mission as to study alleged deprivations of voting rights and alleged discrimination based on race, color, religion, sex, age, disability, or national origin, or in the administration of justice. The International Covenant for Civil and Political Rights, with the UDHR as its base, includes many traditional civil liberties (such as freedom of expression and assembly, and due process) as well as equality provisions (like bans on discriminatory treatment of women), and human rights (the right to dignity and self-determination).

1.4   Defining constitutional rights

The US Constitution, especially in its Bill of Rights and Fourteenth Amendment guarantees of due process and equal protection of the laws, is the ultimate source of protection of American civil liberties as well as the principal codification of America's fundamental values. But the scope of US civil liberties is not necessarily coextensive with constitutional protection. It could be broader or narrower, in theory or in practice. The Constitution sets a floor, but not a ceiling for civil liberties protection. As will be discussed in Chapter 4, the states, sometimes Congress, and sometimes elected officials can take action to protect civil liberties even if they are not implementing a federal constitutional right recognized by the courts.

The scope of the Constitution's provisions, as noted above, is constantly contested. Those who advocate for a generous conception of particular civil liberties may argue that the Constitution should be interpreted more broadly than previous judicial interpretation provides, in addition to looking to other sources for protection. Thus, for example, advocates persuaded the Supreme Court in the *Obergefell* case[2] to declare a federal constitutional right to marriage equality in 2015 (see Section 10.1), when some but not all state courts and legislatures had previously recognized that right. In a very few instances advocates have even succeeded in convincing the Court to impose affirmative constitutional obligations on the government, like provision of counsel to indigent criminal defendants (see Chapter 9). Cases like these show that it is theoretically possible to interpret US constitutional guarantees as going beyond the narrow conception of civil liberties as only negative liberties aimed at preventing tyranny. The decision in *Obergefell* rested in part on a right to dignity and autonomy a majority of the Court derived from the Fourteenth Amendment Due Process Clause.

In a classic statement about the goals of the Constitution, Justice Louis Brandeis described the aims of the Constitution's protections of rights in broad terms:

> The makers of our Constitution … recognized the significance of man's spiritual nature, of his feelings and of his intellect. They knew that only a part

---

2   Obergefell v. Hodges, 576 U.S. 644 (2015).

of the pain, pleasure and satisfactions of life are to be found in material things. They sought to protect Americans in their beliefs, their thoughts, their emotions and their sensations. They conferred, as against the Government, the right to be let alone – the most comprehensive of rights and the right most valued by civilized men.[3]

Even Brandeis's generous conception of the right to be let alone does not encompass anything like the broad panoply of affirmative rights in the UDHR.[4] Eleanor Roosevelt, American champion of the UDHR, and her husband, Franklin Roosevelt, whose ideal Four Freedoms included freedom from want,[5] thought that expanding fundamental American values to include human rights along with civil liberties should be the next American Reconstruction.

---

[3]   Olmstead v. United States, 277 U.S. 438 (1928) (dissenting opinion).
[4]   It has been argued that the Thirteenth and Fourteenth Amendments could be viewed as providing a basis for socioeconomic rights. See Frank Michelman, On Protecting the Poor through the Fourteenth Amendment (1969) 83 *Harvard Law Review* 7; Susan N. Herman, 'Reading between the Lines: Judicial Protection for Socioeconomic Rights Under the South African and United States Constitutions,' in P. Andrews and S. Bazilli (eds), *Comparative Constitutionalism and Rights: Global Perspectives* (Lake Mary FL: Vandeplas, 2008).
[5]   Roosevelt listed freedom of speech, freedom of worship, freedom from want, and freedom from fear as the pillars of human rights.

2 Traditional and documentary origins of US conception and codification of civil liberties

Although the United States of America has always been multicultural, American lawmakers and judges from colonial times through the adoption of the Constitution to the current day have described American law as exclusively derived from English law and common law. This one-dimensional account of Anglo-American tradition glosses over other influences on American law and values. Some historians maintain, for example, that the Constitution's federalist structure was informed by the model of the Iroquois Confederacy. The Civil Code traditions of France and Spain had considerable impact on the laws of Louisiana. Other subliminal influences may be difficult to pinpoint.

But it is unquestionable that the authors of both state and federal constitutions used English law and common law as their principal model – sometimes as a model of rights to replicate and sometimes as an example of evils to avoid by fuller articulation of rights. The US courts adhere to Anglo-American tradition as their North Star in interpreting the Constitution, sometimes nationalizing conceptions of the rights all Americans have regardless of local differences. In *Duncan v. Louisiana*,[1] for example, the Sixth Amendment was held to require Louisiana, despite its significant French heritage and tradition, to conform to a model of the right to jury trial derived from English rather than civil law tradition.

---

[1]   Duncan v. Louisiana, 391 U.S. 145 (1968).

Whether interpretation of the Constitution should ever be influenced by the laws of other countries is an issue that has been vigorously contested. Some American jurists, especially in recent years, have looked to international or comparative law or to international human rights law and principles in interpreting particular provisions of the Constitution. The Eighth Amendment's ban on cruel and unusual punishment, for example, is said to incorporate evolving standards of decency. In a case holding that the Eighth Amendment prohibits execution for a crime committed while a juvenile, Justice Anthony Kennedy found it significant that 'the United States is the only country in the world that continues to give official sanction to the juvenile death penalty.'[2] Dissenting Justice Antonin Scalia bitterly condemned this attention to foreign law as adulterous: 'the basic premise of the Court's argument – that American law should conform to the laws of the rest of the world – ought to be rejected out of hand.'[3]

English tradition is sometimes but not always the tradition most favorable to civil liberties. On the one hand, English tradition does provide jury trials and other procedural guarantees as a check against unjust prosecutions. But on the other hand, Anglo-American tradition sometimes displaced indigenous law that might in some instances have been more conducive to liberty and equality. For example, some Native American tribes like the Navajo and the Rosebud Sioux employed principles of restorative justice rather than punishment for those who violated laws, with the goal of re-establishing harmony in the community. Congress peremptorily rejected that model and superseded tribal law, imposing on the tribes Anglo-American punitive traditions of incarceration and capital punishment which have proven to result in inequitable and oppressive deprivations of liberty.[4] And the libertarian cast of Anglo-American tradition, beginning with Magna Carta, has led American courts to reject constitutional interpretations that would be more conducive to fuller protection of human rights including equality.

---

[2]   Roper v. Simmons, 543 U.S. 551 (2005). Similarly, in finding a statute criminalizing consensual sodomy violative of the Due Process Clause, Kennedy cited the European Court of Human Rights. Lawrence v. Texas, 539 U.S. 558 (2003).

[3]   Roper v. Simmons (Scalia, J., dissenting).

[4]   Major Crimes Act, 18 U.S.C. § 1153 (1885).

2.1   English antecedents: Magna Carta and the rights of Englishmen

Although some English legal concepts have been traced to ancient Roman law or to biblical precepts, the story of English liberties typically begins in 1215 with Magna Carta Libertatum (the Great Charter of Freedoms). English jurist and scholar Edward Coke, whose work was studied by early American scholars, referred to Magna Carta as England's 'ancient constitution.'

While it was not functionally a constitution, Magna Carta significantly limited the power of the sovereign, at least in theory, by establishing: (1) that monarchs must follow the law rather than simply declaring it; (2) that the Church had a right to be free from governmental interference; (3) that all free citizens had a right to own and inherit property and to be protected from excessive taxes; and (4) that the 'law of the land'[5] and some basic principles of justice[6] could prevent the sovereign from depriving individuals of their freedom or their property at will.

Magna Carta was known to many of the American colonists and framers of the US Constitution, but how direct an influence that document actually had on the Constitution has been a subject of debate. The participants in the constitutional convention rarely referred to Magna Carta; the text of the Constitution does not quote any of its provisions. By way of contrast, a number of states did insert passages from Magna Carta, especially 'law of the land' provisions, into their own constitutions or laws.

But even though Magna Carta could be viewed as superseded by the provisions actually written into the Constitution,[7] it is frequently and reverently cited by the US Supreme Court – by one recent count, in

---

5   Clause 39: 'No free man shall be arrested or imprisoned or disseised or outlawed or exiled or in any way victimised, neither will we attack him or send anyone to attack him, except by the lawful judgment of his peers or by the law of the land.'

6   Clause 40: 'To no one will we sell, to no one will we deny or delay right or justice.'

7   In Australia, whose Constitution has no written Bill of Rights, Magna Carta is viewed as an essential referent for claims of liberty.

over 170 opinions.[8] It is invoked by both liberals and conservatives to burnish the historical pedigree of due process rights as well as the autonomy of the Church.[9] Conservatives claim Magna Carta as a source of Anglo-American libertarian tradition preclusive of any interpretation of the Constitution that would serve more progressive or egalitarian aims. Magna Carta was indeed an elitist document. Replete with arcane provisions about medieval property law, it was designed to address the rights and concerns of the nobility. The barons who forced King John to sign this document did not seek to lay the groundwork for republican government; they wanted to be let alone.[10]

The liberties espoused in the thirteenth-century Magna Carta, like the law of the land provision, were not much more than theoretical for centuries. In the seventeenth century, some key Magna Carta principles were incorporated and expanded in significant laws, like the Habeas Corpus Act of 1689, which provided for review of the legality of detention. The 1689 Declaration of Rights, regarded as a direct precedent and model for the US Bill of Rights and for declarations of rights in state constitutions, sharply limited the authority of the monarch by announcing a number of forms of freedom: freedom to elect members of Parliament, without the king or queen's interference; freedom of speech in Parliament; freedom from royal interference with the law; freedom to petition the king; freedom to bear arms for self-defense; freedom from cruel and unusual punishment and excessive bail; freedom from taxation by royal prerogative alone; freedom from fines and forfeitures without a trial; freedom from armies being raised during peacetime.

English common law over the centuries developed protections of property and liberty that were not embodied in either a written Constitution or in statutes. The colonists would have been particularly aware of developments during the 1760s like the judicial imposition of procedural

---

[8]   Stephen Wermiel, 'Magna Carta in Supreme Court Jurisprudence,' in Daniel Magraw et al (eds), *Magna Carta and the Rule of Law* (Chicago, IL: ABA, 2014).

[9]   See, for example, Chief Justice Roberts' opinion in Hosanna-Tabor Evangelical Lutheran Church and School v. Equal Employment Opportunity Commission, 565 U.S. 171 (2012).

[10]   See A.E. Dick Howard, *The Road to Runnymede: Magna Carta and Constitutionalism in America* (Charlottesville: University of Virginia Press, 2015).

limitations on the government's power to conduct searches and seizures[11] and William Blackstone's summary of English law in his Commentaries. Blackstone glorified English protections of liberty – including the 'bulwark' of the right to trial by jury – announcing the liberal principle that it is better to let ten guilty men go free rather than to convict one innocent. But in other areas, like protection of freedom of speech and the press, the framers viewed English common law as providing inadequate protection against royal abuse.

There has been disagreement about how English documents and common law should inform interpretation of the provisions of the Constitution (see Chapter 8). A dissenting Justice in the 1873 *Slaughterhouse Cases*[12] argued that although the original Constitution did not do so, the Fourteenth Amendment's Privileges and Immunities Clause should have been read to protect a broad array of traditional privileges and immunities of Englishmen, described as springing from Magna Carta, against either state or federal government interference: the right of personal security; the right of personal liberty; and the right of private property, including the right to choose one's calling. That position has not found favor with a majority of Justices, although Justice Clarence Thomas has recently argued for a revival of attention to the Privileges and Immunities Clause.[13]

2.2   The Declaration of Independence

The Declaration of Independence is sometimes cited as a source of American values and tradition complementary to the Constitution.

Writing the Declaration of Independence in 1776, Thomas Jefferson followed the format of the English Declaration of Rights. He drew on the work of seventeenth-century English philosophers, especially John Locke, who had posited that all people have an equal, God-given, inalienable right to life, liberty, and property, and that it is necessary to constrain government in order to protect these rights.

---

[11]   Entick v. Carrington, 19 St. Tr. 1030 (1765). See Chapter 8.
[12]   Slaughterhouse Cases, 83 U.S. 36 (1872) (Bradley, J., dissenting).
[13]   See, e.g., McDonald v. City of Chicago, 561 U.S. 742 (2010) (Thomas, J., concurring).

Jefferson adopted some of Locke's language and logic in his introductory paragraphs, including the famous assertion that 'all men are created equal, that they are endowed by their Creator with certain unalienable Rights, that among these are Life, Liberty and the pursuit of Happiness.' The Declaration goes on not to enumerate rights, but to itemize wrongs the colonists complained of suffering at the hands of King George. Those included denials of representation and protection, aggression, and a few examples of denials of fair process ('For depriving us in many cases, of the benefits of Trial by Jury: For transporting us beyond Seas to be tried for pretended offences').

Whether it is fair to rely on the contents of the earlier Declaration of Independence in interpreting the Constitution has been another source of contention.[14]

2.3   The eighteenth-century Constitution

Like its predecessor Articles of Confederation, the 1789 Constitution was devoted to the structures of the federal government rather than to declarations of rights. Only a few rights were specified with respect to the federal government – like the Article III right to trial by jury in federal prosecutions. Framers Alexander Hamilton and James Madison, among others, believed it unnecessary to include a Bill of Rights in the Constitution. Hamilton thought that a declaration of rights was useful in a monarchy but was unnecessary in a republic where the people themselves constitute the government as well as the governed. Madison thought that the checks and balances of the Constitution – both the horizontal check of separation of powers of the three branches of the federal government and the vertical check of federalism – would be sufficient to keep the federal government from despotic actions. But state ratifying conventions pushed back, demanding that the Constitution be amended to include more specific protections against federal overreaching. Madison acceded, due to his concern about the danger of factions and his recognition that, as Edmund Burke had argued, a political majority in a democracy may have both the will and the means to oppress a minority. 'Wherever the real power in

---

[14]   See, e.g., Carlton F. Larson, The Declaration of Independence: A 225th Anniversary Re-Interpretation (2001) 76(3) *Washington Law Review* 701.

a Government lies, there is the danger of oppression,' Madison wrote. 'In our Governments the real power lies in the majority of the Community, and the invasion of private rights is *cheifly* [sic] to be apprehended, not from acts of Government contrary to the sense of its constituents, but from acts in which the Government is the mere instrument of the major number of the constituents.'[15]

The Bill of Rights protections were derived both from negative reactions to the colonists' experience under colonial rule – some rights address grievances like the oppressive use of writs of assistance and denial of jury trial – and from positive examples of the Glorious Revolution Declaration of Rights and common law conceptions of the rights of Englishmen. Like Magna Carta, the Bill of Rights listed negative rights that limit governmental actions, especially actions that would affect the interests of property owners.[16]

What neither the Articles of the Constitution nor the Bill of Rights contained was any mention of equality, despite the noble words of the Declaration of Independence. It would have been the height of hypocrisy to posit equality as a fundamental American value in a document designed to accommodate the institution of slavery.

2.4   The nineteenth-century reconstruction: the Fourteenth Amendment and civil liberties

Cases interpreting and applying the provisions of the Bill of Rights were not numerous in the years before the Civil War. The Bill of Rights applied only to the federal government and federal powers were far more limited than they are today, leaving the states free to order rights, relations, and policy within their own borders. Following the Civil War, the Thirteenth, Fourteenth, and Fifteenth Amendments imposed substantial federal constitutional constraints upon the states, sweeping within the purview

---

15   Letter from James Madison to Thomas Jefferson, October 17, 1788. See https://oll.libertyfund.org/title/madison-the-writings-vol-5-1787-1790.

16   Charles Beard, *An Economic Interpretation of the Constitution* (New York: Simon & Schuster, originally published 1913).

of the federal courts and Congress a vast array of state actions including all criminal prosecutions.

The Fourteenth Amendment's Due Process Clause, prohibiting the states from depriving any person of life, liberty, or property without due process of law, eventually became the conduit for applying most of the Bill of Rights provisions to the states (see Section 4.1). Starting in the mid-twentieth century, the Due Process Clause was held to incorporate substantive as well as procedural rights, including freedom of speech and religion, and to provide a basis for declaring unenumerated rights (like reproductive freedom) to be enforceable against the states as a form of 'substantive due process.' The incorporation and substantive due process decisions vastly expanded the reach of the US Constitution and the federal courts, making US constitutional interpretation a national source of protection for civil liberties.

The Fourteenth Amendment's Equal Protection Clause, providing that no 'State' shall 'deny to any person within its jurisdiction the equal protection of the laws,' was the Constitution's first reference to equality. Equal protection of the laws is a limited form of equality, promising not that all people should be equal, but only that the state will not itself act as a source of unequal treatment.

3 Indelible civil liberties controversies in American history

Events in every era of American history have shown the truth of Madison's prediction that even in a republic without a monarchical tyrant, the civil liberties of minorities will be in danger from political majorities – or from factions wielding political power even if they are not in the majority. Individuals and groups have been deprived of liberties because of their religious or political viewpoints or personal characteristics like national origin, race, or ethnicity when policymakers thought those deprivations would serve the public interest. Most extreme examples of derogation of civil liberties have taken place during times of war or perceived national security crisis. In the name of national security, the United States allowed criminalization of dissenting speech around World War I, curtailed the freedom of loyal Japanese Americans during World War II, and engaged in massive surveillance as part of the 'war on terror.' In hindsight, many actions viewed at the time as patriotic have come to be seen as overreactions, often rooted in bias.

Can we learn from history, or are we condemned to repeat errors, especially during times of perceived crisis?

This section will offer brief accounts of historical incidents frequently recalled in conversations about US civil liberties.

3.1   Early civil liberties challenges: the Alien and Sedition Acts

In 1798, the Federalist Congress was willing to circumscribe the recently exalted freedom of speech by enacting the Sedition Act, which declared it a crime to 'write, print, utter or publish any false, scandalous, and malicious writing' about members of Congress or the president. This Act, complementing the Alien Enemies and Alien Friends Acts, was said to be a necessary precaution in anticipation of war with France. But Federalist prosecutors and judges used the Act to prosecute journalists and politicians of their rival party, Democrat-Republicans, for criticizing their administration. Representative Matthew Lyon, for example, was convicted of sedition and imprisoned for describing the Adams Administration as typified by 'ridiculous pomp, foolish adulation, and selfish avarice.'[1]

The Federalists maintained that the Sedition Act was not inconsistent with the First Amendment's declaration that 'Congress shall make no law … abridging the freedom of speech,' relying on aspects of the British common law's limited conception of that freedom. Many Americans disagreed, arguing that the statute violated central principles of the First Amendment. The states of Virginia and Kentucky adopted resolutions written, respectively, by James Madison and Thomas Jefferson, taking this view and arguing that the federal government should not be the final arbiter of whether its own actions are constitutional.[2]

No one at the time would have expected the Federalist-dominated courts to declare the Sedition Act unconstitutional. Madison and Jefferson looked to federalism as a more likely source of protection of rights, contending that the states should play a role in interpreting the First Amendment and thus in checking the federal government. That view was not accepted, and so the remaining recourse was national politics.

---

[1]   Matthew Lyon, Public Letter (1798), https://founders.archives.gov/documents/Madison/01-17-02-0119#:~:text=scandalous%20and%20seditious%20writing%2C%20or,Smith%2C%20Freedom's%20Fetters%2C%20pp.

[2]   Geoffrey R. Stone, *Perilous Times* (New York: W.W. Norton, 2004).

The Sedition Act provoked widespread anger, contributing to Jefferson's defeat of Adams in the next presidential election. The Sedition Act expired on the last day of the Adams Administration and has been pilloried ever since as an improper attempt to suppress criticism. The Supreme Court has observed that '[although] the Sedition Act was never tested in this Court, the attack upon its validity has carried the day in the court of history.'[3]

3.2   The Civil War

Chief Justice William Rehnquist, in his book *All the Laws but One*, on the history of civil liberties controversies during time of war, concluded that there is considerable truth to the Latin maxim '*inter arma silent leges*' – 'in time of war, the law is silent.'[4]

During the Civil War, President Abraham Lincoln took a number of extreme measures curtailing civil liberties in the interest of winning the war. He suspended the writ of habeas corpus – which allows a judicial challenge to the legality of one's detention – on multiple occasions. Supreme Court Justice Roger Taney, infamous for writing the opinion in the *Dred Scott* case,[5] ruled that the President's act was unconstitutional because the Constitution in Article I Section 9 gives the power to suspend habeas corpus only to Congress.[6] Lincoln told Congress that the Court was wrong and continued to issue orders suspending the writ, without generating much public resistance. Lincoln also authorized military tribunals to try civilians, a practice the Supreme Court also declared to be unconstitutional.[7] It was Lincoln's frustration with judicial second-guessing of his wartime decisions that led him to make the comment Rehnquist used for the title of his book. If he had preserved habeas corpus, Lincoln said, it would have meant allowing 'all the laws,

---

3   New York Times Co. v. Sullivan, 376 U.S. 254 (1964).
4   William H. Rehnquist, *All the Laws but One* (New York: Random House, 1998).
5   Dred Scott v. Sandford, 60 U.S. 393 (1857).
6   *Ex parte* Merryman, 17 F. Cases 144 (D. Md. 1861).
7   *Ex parte* Milligan, 71 U.S. (94 Wall) (1866).

but one, to go unexecuted, and the government itself go to pieces, lest that one [habeas corpus] be violated.'[8]

Lincoln's actions during the Civil War have been debated – as to their actual necessity as well as their constitutionality – but may be regarded as a high water mark of presidential incursion on civil liberties in time of war. And the cases challenging Lincoln's actions were a high water mark of judicial defense of civil liberties even in the face of presidential insistence that constitutionally questionable actions are necessary to promote order and win a war. As Rehnquist observed, the courts have typically been reluctant to rule against the government on issues of national security, especially during wartime.

3.3   World War I era Espionage and Sedition Acts

World War I marked the first time after the expiration of the 1798 Sedition Act that Congress criminalized dissenting and disloyal speech. The Espionage Act of 1917 was proposed three months after the United States entered the war. Following intense debate, Congress narrowed the version initially proposed, deciding to criminalize only obstruction of conscription and registration rather than all disloyal utterances. Later in the war, in 1918, Congress passed an expanded Sedition Act, adding prohibition of willfully uttering or publishing any disloyal language about the form of the US government or the military, or language intended to bring the military into contempt or disrepute. Punishment upon conviction was up to 20 years' imprisonment and a $10,000 fine.

The World War I Espionage and Sedition Acts led to the prosecution and conviction of people who criticized the war, the draft, or the form of government, including Charles Schenck – a socialist who published pamphlets speaking out against the draft on the ground that it amounted to unconstitutional involuntary servitude – and Socialist Party leader Eugene Debs. For their expression of dissenting views, Schenck and Debs were convicted under the Espionage Act for obstructing the draft and received substantial prison sentences. The Supreme Court unanimously upheld these convictions on appeal, rejecting First Amendment chal-

---

[8]   Rehnquist, *All the Laws but One.*

lenges.[9] The *Schenck* opinion, written by Justice Oliver Wendell Holmes, expressed the views of most contemporary lawyers and judges as well as the public that in time of war, the views of the majority about what would constitute disloyalty could override individual freedom of speech. Commentary on the Court's opinions led Holmes to develop his thinking further, as will be described in Section 5.1.

Reaction to abuses around World War I, both repression of dissenting speech and detention of suspected radicals, can be said to have galvanized the modern civil liberties movement. In that era, radical views were generally seen as un-American. The idea that the First Amendment marketplace of ideas is essential to democracy, or that dissent could be patriotic, had not yet captured the public imagination. In 1917, the leaders of the American Union Against Militarism formed a National Civil Liberties Bureau, which several years later became the ACLU, to defend dissidents and conscientious objectors, among others, and to educate the public about the importance of free speech and other civil liberties at a time when the courts were not an ally in that project.

After the war ended, the Sedition Act was repealed and has not been revived, although the 1917 Espionage Act is still in effect.

3.4 World War II

The most traumatic civil liberties controversy during World War II was not about speech but about prejudice against Americans of Japanese ancestry. President Franklin Roosevelt's Executive Order 9066 led to the exclusion of 110,000 Japanese Americans from their West Coast homes and internment of thousands of loyal Japanese Americans. True to Rehnquist's generalization, the Supreme Court deferred to the government's contention that these actions were necessary to prevent a Japanese invasion of the West Coast.[10] Historians subsequently concluded that the

---

[9]   Schenck v. United States, 249 U.S. 47 (1919); Debs v. United States, 249 U.S. 211 (1919). See also Frohwerk v. United States, 249 U.S. 204 (1919).
[10]   Korematsu v. United States, 323 U.S. 214 (1944).

Court's decision had been based on misleading information supplied by the government.[11]

The *Korematsu* decision became an indelible source of national shame. Challengers to President Donald Trump's travel ban targeting Muslims analogized that Executive Order to the biased Executive Order upheld in *Korematsu*. The Supreme Court rejected the comparison and upheld the travel ban, again deferring to a president's controversial claims about national security – but took the occasion to disavow and formally overrule *Korematsu*.[12]

3.5   The red scares

Xenophobia fueled civil liberties crises even after wars ended. The Russian Revolution of 1917 generated alarm that the American form of government would be endangered by anarchists and Communists. Following World War I, US Attorney General A. Mitchell Palmer engaged in a campaign to suppress radicalism that included the so-called Palmer Raids, arresting and deporting thousands of alleged radicals, mostly from Eastern European countries, and detaining, interrogating, and prose-cuting scores of others. Palmer also encouraged states to enact criminal anarchy or syndicalism statutes. These acts, which prohibited advocacy of overthrowing the government, led to the conviction of hundreds of people and the arrest of many more on the basis of their speech and associations.

During the Cold War era of the 1950s, Senator Joseph McCarthy led a vicious red scare campaign, aimed at unmasking and punishing support-ers of Communism. In overheated hearings of the House Un-American Activities Committee, McCarthy pressured people to inform on their friends and colleagues. Prominent Hollywood scriptwriters and actors were among those blacklisted and denied employment because they were believed to have been or to have sympathized with Communists or because they refused to name names. In addition, the McCarthy Era Smith Act, which criminalized advocacy of overthrowing the US govern-

---

[11]   Peter Irons, *Justice at War: The Story of the Japanese-American Internment Cases* (Oakland, CA: University of California Press, 1993).
[12]   Trump v. Hawaii, 585 U.S. ___ (2018).

ment, became the basis for conviction of Communist Party leaders for their advocacy.[13] The courts were slow to react to these threats to freedom of speech and association.

3.6   Post 9/11 'war on terror'

During the 'war on terror' following the events of September 11, 2001, critics who charged the government with anti-Muslim bias in detention and surveillance practices compared those actions to the racist stereotyping of World War II and to the guilt by association of the McCarthy Era,[14] arguing that the US was repeating the same mistakes in a new context. Others argued that the country had learned from its history – at least Muslims were not being subjected to wholesale relocation or internment.

Hundreds of Muslim men were interned, mostly non-Americans who were detained in Guantánamo. In landmark cases reviewing the government's assertion of authority to summarily detain anyone designated as an 'enemy combatant,' the Supreme Court found that the Constitution imposed procedural constraints on depriving individuals, especially US citizens, of their freedom.[15] However, with respect to other challenges to the constitutionality of the government's anti-terrorism campaign, including omnivorous surveillance practices and collaboration in the torture of terrorism suspects,[16] the Court studiously avoided addressing claims on their merits[17] (see Section 4.4), or deferred to the government. In one notable case, the Humanitarian Law Project, a group whose mission

---

[13]   See Dennis v. United States, 341 U.S. 494 (1951). The Court gradually changed First Amendment law to stand up to McCarthyism.

[14]   David Cole, *Enemy Aliens* (New York: New Press, 2005).

[15]   Hamdi v. Rumsfeld, 542 U.S. 507 (2004); Boumediene v. Bush, 553 U.S. 723 (2008).

[16]   Susan N. Herman, *Taking Liberties: The War on Terror and the Erosion of American Democracy* (New York: Oxford University Press, 2014); Anthony Romero and Dina Temple-Raston. *In Defense of Our America: The Fight for Civil Liberties in the Age of Terror* (New York: Harper Collins, 2008).

[17]   See Susan N. Herman, Ab(ju)dication: How Procedure Defeats Civil Liberties in the 'War on Terror' (2017) 50(1) *Suffolk University Law Review* 79. The Court either denied *certiorari* or found procedural reasons not to entertain claims regarding torture and extraordinary rendition, expansive surveillance, harsh treatment of post-9/11 detainees, and so on.

included attempting to persuade terrorists to adopt peaceful means of dispute resolution, contended that a statute criminalizing the provision of 'material support' to terrorists violated their First Amendment freedom of speech when it was interpreted as covering their peacemaking efforts.[18] The Court rejected the First Amendment challenge, announcing that the government was entitled to prohibit anyone – including peacemakers, doctors, or lawyers – from talking with members of a terrorist group because the government claimed that it was a good idea to treat those groups as 'radioactive.' That level of deference to unsupported government theories, as the dissenters noted, was not consistent with previous First Amendment doctrine.

---

[18]   Holder v. Humanitarian Law Project, 561 U.S. 1 (2010).

4   Actualizing civil liberties

Although the scope of civil liberties protection could, as described in Section 1.4, be more extensive than the US Constitution mandates, the Constitution sets a floor for protection of the rights it contains. The Supremacy Clause of Article VI declares that the US Constitution and federal laws and treaties are the supreme law of the land – preempting any policy decisions Congress, the president, and the states might otherwise make. Federal or state governmental actors have discretion to build on that constitutional floor if they wish to be more protective of civil liberties. But this power only goes in one direction – to increase, not to diminish constitutional liberties. Thus, for example, if the Supreme Court rules that the states must respect same-sex marriage, no state can refuse to comply. But before the Court reached the conclusion that marriage equality was a matter of federal constitutional right, a number of state courts or legislatures had declared a right to marry someone of the same sex in their own state – a permissible protection of rights greater than the federal constitutional standard at the time.

The Supreme Court is the focal point for most discussions of civil liberties because it has the power to interpret the Constitution and thus set the least common denominator of rights for the entire nation. This section will begin with an overview of how the Court has used that power to shape US civil liberties.

4.1   The law of civil liberties: an overview

The first case US law students typically study in Constitutional Law is
Marbury v. Madison,[1] where the 1803 Supreme Court announced that
it is 'emphatically the province and duty of the judicial department to
say what the law is.' That pronouncement declared judicial power to say
what the Constitution means even if the ostensibly coequal branches of
government disagree. Judicial review is justified by the fact that in a constitutional democracy, it is the provisions of the Constitution rather than
the preferences of elected officials or voters that are supposed to prevail.

Article III of the Constitution designed the federal courts, including
the Supreme Court, to be sheltered from politics. Federal judges have
life tenure (during 'good Behaviour') and their compensation may not
be diminished during their service, on the theory that they can then be
expected to serve the Constitution rather than their own self-interest.
Politically insulated judges are expected to check even the most popular
governmental actions if those actions, like statutes criminalizing burning
a flag in a protest or imposing draconian treatment on sex offenders,
violate constitutional precepts. Constitutional democracy means that
the Constitution trumps democracy. But judicial review has also been
criticized for what Alexander Bickel called its counter-majoritarian difficulty. Unelected judges could subvert democracy by using their power to
declare laws unconstitutional in service of their own beliefs.

Around the turn of the twentieth century, in what came to be known as
the *Lochner* Era, the Supreme Court regularly found progressive laws to
be unconstitutional in part because the Justices regarded those laws as
inconsistent with laissez-faire economic policy. In the 1905 *Lochner* case
itself, for example, the Court invalidated a state labor law regulating the
working hours of bakers, on the ground that it unreasonably interfered
with a liberty of contract the Court derived from the Due Process Clause
– a substantive due process ruling.[2] The majority's economic views, which
they read into the Constitution, were out of sync with the views of most
Americans and stymied what some count as hundreds of federal and state
legislative attempts to regulate markets. Backlash to the Court's intransi-

---

[1]   Marbury v. Madison, 5 U.S. 137 (1803).
[2]   Lochner v. New York, 198 U.S. 45 (1905).

gence peaked in 1937 when President Franklin Roosevelt, frustrated that five unelected Justices were blocking economic measures he and Congress believed necessary to lift the country out of the Great Depression, threatened to neutralize the Court by packing it with additional Justices. Whether or not in response to that threat, that same year one Justice changed his course and cast a critical fifth vote to uphold labor laws and other economic policies – a decision humorously known as the 'switch in time that saved the nine.'

In a 1938 case called *Carolene Products*, the Court, continuing to renounce the excesses of the *Lochner* Era, declined to strike down a rather foolish federal statute protecting consumers from the purported evils of a product known as filled milk. In addition to explaining why the courts should ordinarily defer to the policy decisions of elected officials, the Court also articulated in a footnote – the now famed Footnote 4 – a theory of the circumstances under which more aggressive judicial review might be appropriate:

> There may be narrower scope for operation of the presumption of constitutionality when legislation appears on its face to be within a specific prohibition of the Constitution, such as those of the first ten Amendments, which are deemed equally specific when held to be embraced within the Fourteenth.
>
> It is unnecessary to consider now whether legislation which restricts those political processes which can ordinarily be expected to bring about repeal of undesirable legislation, is to be subjected to more exacting judicial scrutiny under the general prohibitions of the Fourteenth Amendment than are most other types of legislation.
>
> Nor need we enquire whether similar considerations enter into the review of statutes directed at particular religious, or national, or racial minorities, whether prejudice against discrete and insular minorities may be a special condition, which tends seriously to curtail the operation of those political processes ordinarily to be relied upon to protect minorities, and which may call for a correspondingly more searching judicial inquiry.[3]

Footnote 4 suggests that the courts have a special role to play with respect to fundamental rights, suspect classifications, and obstacles to democratic participation – as opposed to routine decisions about social, health, and economic policy which are to be made by elected officials who have what is sometimes called the police power. That idea shaped judicial review of

---

[3]   United States v. Carolene Products Company, 304 U.S. 144 (1938).

constitutional claims throughout the rest of the twentieth century and beyond.

The Fourteenth Amendment Due Process Clause allowed the Supreme Court to review the procedural fairness of state actions including criminal proceedings. Chapter 9 will describe how the Supreme Court occasionally used this power during the first half of the twentieth century to reverse grossly unjust state criminal convictions. Beginning in the 1940s, the Court decided to go beyond that case-by-case approach, finding that the Due Process Clause, in addition to requiring process generally regarded as fair, also incorporated most of the provisions of the Bill of Rights. The Court's decisions bound the states to follow almost all of the same rules as the federal government with respect to freedom of speech, freedom of religion, search and seizure, right to trial by jury, and criminal procedure.

In addition to using incorporation to extend the territorial reach of rights, the famously liberal Warren Court interpreted the underlying Bill of Rights provisions themselves quite expansively. During the 1960s, the Fourth Amendment right to be free from unreasonable searches and seizures was found to require state as well as federal courts to exclude from criminal trials evidence obtained in violation of Fourth Amendment requirements (the exclusionary rule);[4] the Fifth Amendment privilege against self-incrimination prohibited use of confessions obtained during custodial interrogation not preceded by *Miranda* warnings;[5] and the Sixth Amendment right to counsel required states to provide free representation to criminal defendants who could not afford to hire an attorney.[6] As will be described in Chapter 9, the Warren Court seemed to regard procedural protections not just as a matter of fairness, but also as an antidote to unequal justice.

Under the auspices of Footnote 4's representation-reinforcement theory (assuming judicial responsibility for addressing obstacles to equal political participation),[7] the Warren Court also closely scrutinized limitations

---

[4]   Mapp v. Ohio, 367 U.S. 643 (1961).

[5]   Miranda v. Arizona, 384 U.S. 486 (1966).

[6]   Gideon v. Wainwright, 372 U.S. 335 (1963).

[7]   See John Hart Ely, *Democracy and Distrust: A Theory of Judicial Review* (Cambridge, MA: Harvard University Press, 1981) (a powerful defense of representation-reinforcement theory).

on the right to vote and unequal weighting of individual votes, forcing the states to adopt more inclusive and egalitarian policies (see Chapter 12).

From the 1970s to the 2000s, the changing composition of the Court, headed by William Rehnquist starting in 1986, led to substantial retrenchment in some areas, including erection of higher procedural barriers to federal constitutional litigation (see Sections 4.3 and 4.4). But during this era, especially during the earlier years, the Court also continued to generate some landmark protections of rights, including procedural due process rights in civil contexts[8] and the decision to have an abortion in *Roe v. Wade*.[9] Moderate Justices, especially Anthony Kennedy and Sandra Day O'Connor (the first woman on the Court), brokered compromises on controversial issues of rights and equality, including preserving the 'essential core of *Roe v. Wade*' in a 1992 case (see Section 10.4), and establishing fact-based rules about when affirmative action policies would be allowed (see Chapter 11). The Court was unusually stable toward the end of this period, with the same nine Justices serving together from 1994 to 2005.

In 2005, John Roberts was appointed Chief Justice by President George W. Bush. Roberts was expected to side with the most conservative members of the Court (Clarence Thomas and Samuel Alito). But his unique role as Chief Justice led him to seek to protect the Court's reputation for being apolitical, including by sometimes advocating respect for precedent rather than voting his own politics. Many were surprised, for example, when he supplied the deciding vote to uphold the Affordable Care Act (a.k.a. Obamacare) in 2012, and to strike down a Louisiana anti-abortion law in a 2020 case.

For the first two decades of the twenty-first century, the Court continued the Footnote 4 tradition of closing scrutinizing and frequently striking down limitations on freedoms regarding as fundamental, including the freedom of speech and an expanded category of implied individual privacy and autonomy rights. In 2003, the Court struck down state statutes that criminalized consensual sodomy[10] and in 2015 voided state

---

8   Goldberg v. Kelly, 397 U.S. 254 (1970); Mathews v. Eldridge, 424 U.S. 319 (1976).
9   Roe v. Wade, 410 U.S. 113 (1973).
10 Lawrence v. Texas, 539 U.S. 558 (2003).

statutes defining marriage as unavailable to same-sex couples[11] (see Chapter 10).

Starting in late 2020, three highly conservative Justices appointed by Donald Trump (Neil Gorsuch, Brett Kavanaugh, and Amy Coney Barrett) shifted the Court's center of gravity, creating a block of five conservative votes not dependent on Roberts. The new Court's highest profile change in constitutional interpretation was to uphold a Mississippi anti-abortion law on the ground that *Roe v. Wade* had been wrong to find that abortion involved a fundamental constitutional right (see Chapter 10). This decision provoked speculation about whether the Court might also rescind constitutional protection for contraception, same-sex marriage, or other rights not explicitly enumerated in the Constitution, an extreme position Justice Clarence Thomas espoused in his concurring opinion.

Minimizing the doctrine of *stare decisis* (respect for the Court's precedents), the Court also expanded the scope of enumerated rights it favored. A divided Court in 2008 had disregarded precedent and interpreted the Second Amendment to guarantee an individual right to bear arms, providing individuals with a constitutional basis for challenging gun control laws a majority of Americans approved.[12] The Court then expanded that right in 2022.[13] The First Amendment rights to free speech and freedom of religion became even more favored rights. For example, the Court became more sympathetic to the argument that the religion clauses of the First Amendment may provide a constitutional defense to people who claim a religious basis for refusing to comply with anti-discrimination laws or who wish to pray at a public school occasion (see Chapter 7).

The twenty-first century Court, beginning during the tenure of Justices Kennedy and O'Connor, also reconfigured Footnote 4's category of suspect classifications. Rather than providing special judicial scrutiny only on behalf of members of discrete and insular minority groups which historically had been subjected to discriminatory laws, the Court decided

---

[11]   Obergefell v. Hodges, 576 U.S. 644 (2015).

[12]   District of Columbia v. Heller, 554 U.S. 570 (2008); McDonald v. Chicago, 561 U.S. 742 (2010).

[13]   New York Rifle and Pistol Association v. Bruen, 597 U.S. ___ (2022) invalidated a New York law imposing limits on the right to carry a weapon in public.

to strictly scrutinize all racial classifications, including those aimed at redressing past discrimination, as discussed in Section 11.3. Entertaining claims on behalf of white people complaining of racial discrimination on the basis of *their* race led the Court to outlaw some, although not all, affirmative action measures[14] as well as race-conscious attempts to integrate schools.[15] See Section 11.3. Court-watchers predicted that after 2022, the Court would continue to radically change settled law in areas like affirmative action and religion, and in recalibrating the level of judicial deference afforded federal administrative agencies.

Through the first two decades of the twenty-first century, the Court also abandoned the third Footnote 4 category – representation reinforcement. Instead of strictly scrutinizing repressive laws, the Court deferred to state laws making the right to vote less equal,[16] eviscerated landmark congressional protections of voting rights,[17] and announced that it would not review state legislative gerrymandering decisions that locked in the power of a minority of voters to choose a majority of federal and state legislators[18] (see Chapter 12).

Polls showed that a majority, and often a supermajority, of Americans disagreed with the Court's choices on issues like abortion and gun control. State legislatures, which are able to use gerrymandering and election rules to protect incumbents and preserve minority rule, are the least democratic elected bodies in the country. So by shrinking federal rights and channeling power to the state legislatures, the Court was preventing a majority of Americans from promoting rights, lowering rather than raising the floor for many civil liberties protections, and blocking popular

---

[14]   Gratz v. Bollinger, 539 U.S. 244 (2003).
[15]   Parents Involved in Community Schools v. Seattle School District No. 1, 551 U.S. 701 (2007).
[16]   Crawford v. Marion County Election Board, 553 U.S. 181 (2008) (upholding a state voter identification law the state justified as an anti-fraud measure even though there was no evidence of in-person voter fraud in that state and scant evidence elsewhere).
[17]   Brnovich v. Democratic National Committee, 594 U.S. ___ (2021) (minimizing the impact of the provision of the 1965 Voting Rights Act remaining after the Court had already disabled the Act's other critical protections in Shelby County v. Holder, 570 U.S. 529 (2013)).
[18]   Rucho v. Common Cause, 588 U.S. ___ (2019).

gun control and civil rights laws by declaring them to infringe favored rights.[19]

In many respects, the Court had come full circle from the *Lochner* Era Court, grafting conservative politics onto constitutional interpretation.

Chapters 5–12 will discuss the law in particular areas in greater depth, starting with the First Amendment.

4.2   Dynamics of judicial interpretation

The Footnote 4 template requires a court confronting a constitutional claim to first decide what level of scrutiny is to be applied. Where laws or government actions infringe fundamental rights or rest on a suspect classification, a reviewing court is to use 'strict scrutiny': the governmental action in question is presumed unconstitutional; the government has the burden of showing that the interest it wishes to serve is 'compelling' and also that the means employed are the least restrictive alternative available to serve that compelling interest. If no fundamental right or suspect classification is involved, the challenged governmental action will be presumed constitutional and the courts will ask only if the action is rationally related to a legitimate governmental interest. In cases applying low-level rational basis scrutiny, the plaintiff bears a very heavy burden in trying to persuade a court not to defer to elected officials' policy choices.

The tests applied on both tiers of review are balancing tests, balancing the individual's claim of right against the state's goal of promoting what is said to be the public interest – but the two tests are heavily weighted in opposite directions. When strict scrutiny is applied the government is only rarely found able to meet its burden, so the decision to apply strict scrutiny usually results in a victory for the challenger. When the bottom tier rational basis review is applied, on the other hand, challengers almost always lose.

---

[19]   See Pamela Karlan et al, Symposium: The New Countermajoritarian Difficulty (2021) 109(6) *California Law Review*; Miriam Seifter, Countermajoritarian Legislatures (2021) 121(6) *Columbia Law Review*.

Within this basic framework, the Court has also developed intermediate levels of scrutiny. While racial classifications receive strict scrutiny, classifications on the basis of sex receive intermediate scrutiny, requiring only that the government show that its action is substantially related to an important interest.[20] The Court has also identified some categories of speech that receive strict scrutiny and other categories, like commercial speech, that receive a more lenient form of scrutiny (see Section 5.8).

In recent years, some Justices have resisted the hierarchical frameworks of Footnote 4. Anthony Kennedy, for example, avoided the question of what level of scrutiny to apply to discrimination on the basis of sexual orientation by developing an alternative theory based on animus.[21] In recent years, the Court has shown a preference for history-based approaches[22] rather than utilizing tiers of scrutiny, leaving the future of this aspect of Footnote 4 theory uncertain.

4.3   State action

The Supreme Court has also developed a number of doctrines that frequently excuse courts from considering the merits of civil liberties claims.

First is the doctrine of state action. The Bill of Rights, Due Process Clause, and Equal Protection Clause of the US Constitution – the major sources of federal constitutional protection for civil liberties – have all been interpreted as applying only to governmental and not to private actions. The First Amendment begins, 'Congress shall make no law,' Section 1 of the Fourteenth Amendment begins, 'No State shall …'

By narrowly defining state action, courts wishing to do so can minimize protection for constitutional liberties and equality, either from Congress or from the courts themselves. When the nineteenth-century Congress used its new Fourteenth Amendment enforcement power to prohibit

---

[20]   Craig v. Boren, 429 U.S. 190 (1976).
[21]   See Romer v. Evans, 517 U.S. 620 (1996).
[22]   In developing Second Amendment law, for example, the Court focused on history and did not identify a tier of scrutiny. New York State Rifle & Pistol Association, Inc. v. Bruen, 597 U.S. ___ (2022).

racial segregation in privately owned establishments like restaurants, for example, the Supreme Court announced that Congress was not appropriately enforcing the Equal Protection Clause because that clause does not apply to private actors.[23]

The state action doctrine has served to limit the volume of constitutional litigation over issues like procedural due process. The Court has held, for example, that a public utilities company, even if it enjoys monopoly status, was not acting on behalf of the state and thus did not have to provide due process or equal protection to its customers.[24] Such decisions leave more leeway for states and private companies to adopt policies that might be unfair or discriminatory.

The state action requirement is one of the chief features distinguishing American civil liberties law from a human rights model, which would focus more on individual entitlement than on state causation of harm.

4.4   Justiciability and procedural limitations

Similarly, the Court employs a wide variety of justiciability doctrines and procedural rulings to control the flow of constitutional decision-making.

Standing is one of the most important of these valves. The standing doctrine holds that people may not bring a lawsuit in federal court unless they can show that they personally have been injured by the action they want to challenge. This limitation, based on the specification in Article III of the Constitution that the federal courts may hear only 'cases' or 'controversies,' has been taken to mean that the federal courts should not render advisory opinions about the constitutionality of legislation or other governmental actions. The courts are required to wait until a case or controversy exists. The Supreme Court has chosen to define the standing requirement as imposing numerous obstacles, thus closing the doors of the courthouse to constitutional questions the courts might prefer not to entertain. The Supreme Court held, for instance, that in order to challenge the constitutionality of a covert surveillance program, plaintiffs must

---

[23]   Civil Rights Cases, 109 U.S. 3 (1883).
[24]   Jackson v. Metropolitan Edison Company, 419 U.S. 345 (1974).

establish that they were actually subjected to covert surveillance – not merely that they feared they were or that it was likely that they were being surveilled.[25] This catch-22 insulates what may be questionable surveillance practices, since the essence of covert surveillance is that targets are not informed that they are under surveillance. The courts also declined to consider challenges to the legality of detentions at Guantánamo by anyone other than a detainee or their family member.[26] While detainees were being held incommunicado, that condition made challenges nearly impossible.

Employing a wide variety of other preclusive procedural doctrines – the political question doctrine, the state secrets privilege, pleading requirements, etc. – the federal courts managed to avoid considering the merits of multiple highly credible claims that people being interrogated in connection with terrorism investigations had been tortured, even when those people brought lawsuits on their own behalf[27] and even when the rights of an American citizen were involved[28] (see Section 3.6).

Finally, as a practical matter, the Supreme Court has almost complete control over its docket because it is able to choose whether or not to hear a case by deciding whether or not to grant what is called a writ of *certiorari*. Thus the Court can simply ignore issues it does not wish to confront and control the timing of hearing the issues it does wish to consider.

4.5   Governmental officials' shared responsibility for implementing constitutional rights

Beyond the Supreme Court, US civil liberties rise and fall depending on the actions of a highly intricate network of actors.

---

25   Clapper v. Amnesty International, 568 U.S. 398 (2013).
26   Coalition of Clergy, Lawyers, and Professors v. Bush, 310 F.3d 1153 (9th Cir. 2002). The Supreme Court denied *certiorari*: 538 U.S. 1031 (2003).
27   See Susan N. Herman, Ab(ju)dication: How Procedure Defeats Civil Liberties in the 'War on Terror' (2017) 50(1) *Suffolk University Law Review* 79.
28   Meshal v. Higgenbotham, 804 F.3d 417 (DC Cir. 2015), *cert. denied* 2017.

Under Article VI of the US Constitution, federal and state officials in all three branches of government – legislative, executive, and judicial – are required to take an oath to uphold the Constitution. Since government, as described above, poses the chief threat to civil liberties, it may seem ironic that the actualization of rights is often dependent on governmental actors. This can be a source of strength, however, especially in eras when the courts under-define civil liberties.

Congress. The post-Civil War amendments to the Constitution – including the Thirteenth Amendment abolition of slavery; the Fourteenth Amendment ban on state due process violations and denials of equal protection of the laws; and the Fifteenth Amendment ban on racial discrimination with respect to voting – all explicitly gave Congress authority to enforce those guarantees. Congress has had a mixed record in using those powers to promote civil rights and civil liberties, sometimes making painfully slow progress. It was only after allowing almost a century of racist voter suppression that Congress finally enacted a powerful Voting Rights Act in 1965. Thousands of Black men were lynched in the nineteenth and twentieth centuries, but Congress did not manage to enact a law banning lynching until 2022.

Further, the Supreme Court has claimed the prerogative to review Congress's enforcement decisions. As discussed in Chapter 7, the Court limits Congress to enforcing only rights the Supreme Court has recognized and not, for example, generally expanding religious freedom or equality.[29] The Court's rollback of key provisions of the Voting Rights Act (see Chapter 12) shows that Congress's power to promote civil liberties, even when it musters the political will to do so, is not boundless.

Federal agencies, especially the US Department of Justice, have a special role to play in implementing federal civil rights and civil liberties statutes. In fact, the civil liberties movement of the early twentieth century was inspired in part by progressives within government who became concerned about the growing power of the administrative state and wanted

---

[29]　See City of Boerne v. Flores, 521 U.S. 507 (1997) (voiding the Religious Freedom Restoration Act of 1993 (RFRA) because it created new rights for religious entities).

authority to protect civil liberties.[30] The Equal Employment Opportunity Commission, to take one example, has authority to implement federal civil rights statutes respecting employment that go considerably beyond constitutional equality rights. But here too, the courts can exercise their powers to check decisions to promote civil liberties – increasingly often on the ground that Congress has not clearly authorized particular executive actions.

States have the power to expand constitutional rights through their own constitutions and statutes, but not to curtail federally recognized rights – a one way ratchet. Massachusetts, for example, recognized a right to same-sex marriage years before the Supreme Court did.[31] From the time of the Virginia and Kentucky resolutions described in Section 3.1, however, state officials have held very different views of what their oath to uphold the US Constitution means. A number of state legislatures enacted statutes inconsistent with the rights recognized in *Roe v. Wade* long before that case was overruled, with some arguing that the states had the right to adopt their own view of the meaning of the Constitution rather than deferring to the Supreme Court's interpretation. The extremist 'constitutional sheriffs' claim that both federal and state law should be subordinated to local law enforcement discretion. The platform presented to the Texas Republican Party in 2022 announced that the state should have the prerogative of nullifying federal judicial decisions it regarded as overreaching.

When enforcement decisions are left to state and local entities rather than federalized, protection of civil liberties, whether the ability to obtain an abortion or freedom from arbitrary search or arrest, is a veritable patchwork, with one's civil liberties index depending on where in the country one lives.

---

[30]   Jeremy K. Kessler, The Administrative Origins of Modern Civil Liberties Law (2014) 114 *Columbia Law Review*.
[31]   Goodridge v. Dept. of Public Health, 798 N.E.2d 941 (Mass. 2003).

4.6   Non-governmental organizations

A wide variety of organizations in the United States promote civil rights or civil liberties positions through lobbying, litigation, and public education. It is impossible to know what the status of civil liberties in the United States would be if these organizations did not exist. David Cole refers to citizen activists and the non-governmental organizations in which they combine their efforts as 'Engines of Liberty.'[32]

The National Association for the Advancement of Colored People (NAACP) is America's oldest and largest civil rights organization. Established in 1909, the organization has fought both private and law enforcement violence against Black people, racial segregation – most famously in its carefully orchestrated campaign to end racial segregation in public schools in a long series of cases apotheosized in *Brown v. Board of Education*[33] – and racial discrimination in a wide variety of guises.

The ACLU, as mentioned in Section 3.3, was born in a turbulent era of xenophobia and suppression of speech around World War I. The ACLU is best known for being the most frequent litigator in the Supreme Court – other than the federal government – but the ACLU initially promoted the values of freedom of speech and due process through pamphlets and other forms of public education because the courts were not receptive to such claims in that era. Throughout the early twentieth century, the ACLU helped to promote judicial review of First Amendment claims – which served as a springboard for the development of other rights.[34]

Many other organizations in the United States have missions overlapping with the NAACP and ACLU. Some, like the Center for Constitutional Rights, also champion a wide variety of civil rights and liberties. Others focus on particular issues – like Planned Parenthood advocating for

---

[32]   David Cole, *Engines of Liberty: The Power of Citizen Activists to Make Constitutional Law* (New York: Basic Books, 2016) (chronicling individual and organizational campaigns to get the law to recognize rights in three sample areas: same sex marriage, gun rights, and human rights in the 'war on terror').

[33]   Brown v. Board of Education, 347 U.S. 483 (1954).

[34]   Ellis Cose, *Democracy, If We Can Keep It: The ACLU's 100-Year Fight for Rights in America* (New York: The New Press, 2020).

reproductive rights; the Lambda Legal Defense Fund and the Human Rights Campaign advocating for LGBTQ rights; the Electronic Frontier Foundation; the Brennan Center for Justice, etc. Other organizations – like the Thomas More Law Center (promoting Judeo-Christian rights); the American Center for Law and Justice; and the American Constitutional Rights Union – vie for a more conservative vision of civil liberties that would feature greater protection of religious liberty, free speech, and the rights of gun owners. Human rights and civil rights organizations – like Human Rights Watch, Human Rights First, and Amnesty International – also pursue missions overlapping civil liberties.

International coalition. The ACLU is part of a collaborative International Network of Civil Liberties Organizations (INCLO)[35] which, since 2013, has issued reports on the worldwide status of civil liberties in four areas: Protest Rights and Policing, Surveillance and Human Rights, Religious Freedom and Equal Treatment, and Protecting Civic Space. Defining civil liberties on a global level can raise challenging questions about the extent to which US conceptions of civil liberties are international as opposed to contingent on US history and values choices. Not all countries share the same views, for example, on whether hate speech or disrespect for national symbols may be prohibited.[36]

---

[35]   The American Civil Liberties Union (United States), Association for Civil Rights in Israel, Canadian Civil Liberties Association, Centro de Estudios Legales y Sociales (Argentina), Dejusticia (Colombia), Egyptian Initiative for Personal Rights, Human Rights Law Centre (Australia), Human Rights Law Network (India), Hungarian Civil Liberties Union, International Human Rights Group Agora (Russia), Irish Council for Civil Liberties, Kenya Human Rights Commission, KontraS (Indonesia), Legal Resources Centre (South Africa), and Liberty (United Kingdom).

[36]   France and Germany, for example, have laws providing punishment for categories of hate speech and for denying the reality of the Holocaust.

PART II

US civil liberties: highlights and examples

5   Freedom of speech and the First Amendment

5.1   Development of judicial protection of speech

It is no coincidence that freedom of speech and its correlative liberties appear at the top of the Bill of Rights. James Madison described freedom of speech and press as 'those choicest privileges of the people.'[1] But in composing the Bill of Rights, the framers left few clues as to how broad they intended the freedom of speech to be. As a matter of history, English law sometimes served as a positive model, as in its antipathy to prior restraint of speech. But, according to First Amendment champion Hugo Black, there was a 'generally accepted belief that one of the objects of the Revolution was to get rid of the English common law on liberty of speech and of the press,'[2] including plaintiff-friendly libel laws.

Different constituencies have offered a variety of rationales for the framers' decision to give primacy to these rights: as a check on tyranny; as a statement of the relationship of the individual and the state; as a bulwark of democracy; as a prerequisite for democratic government. These rationales can sometimes point in different directions. In the examples to follow, note how results are frequently dictated by a court's selection of one rationale rather than another, as well as by the elements the courts have prescribed in their construction of First Amendment doctrine – like

---

[1]   James Madison, Speech Introducing Proposed Constitutional Amendments (1789). See https://oll.libertyfund.org/page/1789-madison-speech-introducing-proposed-amendments-to-the-constitution.

[2]   Bridges v. California, 314 U.S. 252 (1941).

categorizing different forms of speech correlated with different balancing tests.

One important feature to note about the Bill of Rights generally is that it targeted only the federal government: 'Congress shall make no law … abridging the freedom of speech.' The authors saw the federal government, like the English monarchy they had recently overthrown, as a threat to civil liberties because it was more distant from the people than local governments. This left the states almost entirely free to make their own decisions about the scope of rights, including of freedom of speech. The 1919 sedition cases discussed here involved federal prosecutions. But in 1925, in the case of *Gitlow v. New York*,[3] the Court decided that the Fourteenth Amendment should be deemed to have 'incorporated' the First Amendment freedom of speech, and so any constitutional constraints on government suppression of speech have also applied to the states since then.

The First Amendment freedom of speech was also the first frontier for twentieth-century expansion of judicial protection of civil liberties. The story of how this happened typically focuses on the intellectual journey of two Supreme Court Justices: Oliver Wendell Holmes and Louis Brandeis.[4] In 1919, the Supreme Court unanimously had allowed convictions of World War I dissidents to stand (see Section 3.3), but Holmes and Brandeis became troubled by the legal concepts propounded in those cases, including Holmes's own 'clear and present danger' test. Holmes had declared in the *Schenck* case, as the Court has held ever since, that despite the absolute language of the First Amendment ('Congress shall make no law …') the freedom of speech is not absolute: 'the most stringent protection of free speech would not protect a man in falsely shouting fire in a theater and causing panic.'[5] By analogy, Holmes had reasoned that speech urging people to resist the draft posed a clear and present danger to the war effort and thus was not entitled to protection under the First Amendment. The clear and present danger test may sound like a strong

---

[3]   Gitlow v. New York, 268 U.S. 652 (1925).
[4]   See Richard Polenberg, *Fighting Faiths: The Abrams Case, the Supreme Court, and Free Speech* (Ithaca, NY: Cornell University Press, 1999).
[5]   Schenck v. United States, 249 U.S. 47 (1919).

protection for rights, but as Robert Cover has noted, that view is mislead-ing.[6] The test was born as an apology for repression.

Holmes and Brandeis decided to dissent in a later 1919 case, *Abrams v. United States*,[7] where the Espionage Act had been used against defend-ants who were charged with disseminating pamphlets warning workers that the munitions they were making might be used against America's World War I ally, Russia, rather than Germany. Their dissent articulated several principles that the Court eventually accepted as First Amendment gospel.[8] First, even in times of war, 'the principle of the right to free speech is always the same.'

> [W]hen men have realized that time has upset many fighting faiths, they may come to believe even more than they believe in the very foundations of their own conduct that the ultimate good desired is better reached by free trade in ideas – that the best test of truth is the power of the thought to get itself accepted in the competition of the marketplace.[9]

It is 'only the present danger of immediate evil or an intent to bring it about that warrants Congress in setting a limit to the expression of opinion.' Rather than allowing suppression of speech if it was deemed to have a bad tendency or to pose a clear and present danger, Holmes's *Abrams* formulation focused on the imminence of harm. People should be free to express unpopular opinions 'unless they so imminently threaten immediate interference with the lawful and pressing purpose of the law that an immediate check is required to save the country.' The best anti-dote to bad speech, in this view, is usually more speech – not suppression.

Holmes and Brandeis themselves modeled the value of the dissenting voice. In the earlier cases, the Court's acceptance of punishing dissident speech had been unanimous, seemingly accepting the premise of the Espionage and Sedition Laws that it would be disloyal not to present a united front in time of war. The very existence of a dissenting opinion about antiwar speech in a 1919 Supreme Court case was a harbinger of

---

[6]   Robert M. Cover, The Left, the Right and the First Amendment: 1918–1928 (1981) 40(3) *Maryland Law Review* 349.

[7]   Abrams v. United States, 250 U.S. 616 (1919).

[8]   Richard Polenberg, *Fighting Faiths: The Abrams Case, the Supreme Court, and Free Speech* (Ithaca, NY: Cornell University Press, 1999).

[9]   Abrams v. United States, 250 U.S. 616 (1919) (dissenting opinion).

a new role for the Court: protecting the right to dissent rather than simply deferring to jingoistic claims of patriotism. Over the next few decades, Supreme Court majority opinions came to embrace the idea that the courts should set a high bar for government suppression or punishment of speech.

The Supreme Court's most ringing statement of its newfound First Amendment orthodoxy came in a 1943 case involving a West Virginia requirement that all schoolchildren salute the flag as a symbol of national solidarity and patriotism. The Court had previously upheld a flag salute requirement in a 1940 case, by a resounding eight to one vote.[10] But when the Barnette family, Jehovah's Witnesses, challenged the constitutionality of the West Virginia law, the Court by a vote of six to three overruled its earlier decision even though only a few years had passed.[11]

Remarkably, *West Virginia State Board of Education v. Barnette* was decided while World War II was still raging. Holding that the Barnettes had the right to decline to perform this gesture of patriotism, Justice Robert Jackson's majority opinion celebrated the American ideal of individual liberty – what the country was defending against totalitarian enemies – rather than the flag itself.

> If there is any fixed star in our constitutional constellation, it is that no official, high or petty, can prescribe what shall be orthodox in matters of politics, nationalism, religion, or other matters of opinion or force citizens to confess by word their faith therein.
>
> The very purpose of a Bill of Rights was to withdraw certain subjects from the vicissitudes of political controversy, to place them beyond the reach of majorities and officials and to establish them as legal principles to be applied by the courts. One's right to life, liberty, and property, to free speech, a free press, freedom of worship and assembly, and other fundamental rights may not be submitted to vote; they depend on the outcome of no elections.

In some ways, the country had come a long way from World War I. West Virginia's opinion about the importance of patriotic observances and national unity during wartime did not seem compelling either to the Court or to Congress. No sedition act punishing antiwar speech was adopted during World War II – perhaps because that war was far more

---

[10]   Minersville School District v. Gobitis, 310 U.S. 586 (1940).
[11]   West Virginia Bd. of Ed. v. Barnette, 319 U.S. 624 (1943).

popular than World War I had been and so it seemed less necessary to police loyalty.

Like Brandeis's declaration of a constitutional 'right to be let alone' (see Section 8.3), *Barnette* is frequently cited in briefs and opinions for the proposition that a central purpose of constitutional rights is to carve out a private sphere for individual liberty against the wishes of the majority. The case also reinforced the primacy of the Court's role as guardian of that sphere against elected officials.

5.2   The *Brandenburg* test

First Amendment cases frequently involve unpopular minorities, as governments are unlikely to try to suppress popular or mainstream viewpoints. The Barnette family were Jehovah's Witnesses, whose religious views were not widely understood or respected.[12] First Amendment controversies in the first part of the twentieth century involved antiwar activists, anarchists, labor organizers, socialists, and Communists, all of whom were widely regarded as radicals threatening public order.

The case in which the Court crystallized its free speech doctrine, *Brandenburg v. Ohio*[13] in 1969, involved the hateful speech of a member of the Ku Klux Klan. Clarence Brandenburg was convicted under an Ohio syndicalism law for expressing racist and antisemitic views at a rally he had organized. His virulent remarks endorsed the prospect of white supremacist violence. He told those assembled 'that there might have to be some revengeance [sic] taken' for the 'continued suppression of the white, Caucasian race.'

---

[12]   Jehovah's Witnesses believe that bowing down to a flag or saluting it is a religious act that ascribes the power of salvation to the State rather than to God.
[13]   Brandenburg v. Ohio, 395 U.S. 444 (1969).

The *Brandenburg* Court, disavowing the laxer clear and present danger test of earlier cases, drew a line between mere advocacy and incitement:

> even speech advocating the use of force or illegal conduct is protected under the First Amendment unless the advocacy is directed to inciting or producing imminent lawless action and is likely to incite or produce such action.

The *Brandenburg* test is difficult for the government to satisfy because it has multiple elements: speech must *intentionally* and *effectively* provoke a crowd to *immediately* carry out violent and unlawful action. Imposing such a heavy burden on state or federal government before they may restrict or punish speech follows Robert Jackson's lead in shifting power from government to the individual to decide what speech will enter the marketplace of ideas. As the ACLU has explained on its website, 'The First Amendment's robust protections in this context reflect two fundamentally important values. First, political advocacy – rhetoric meant to inspire action against unjust laws or policies – is essential to democracy. Second, people should be held accountable for their own conduct, regardless of what someone else may have said.'[14]

5.3   'Hate speech' and content neutrality

It may seem surprising that the ACLU agreed to represent Clarence Brandenburg despite sharply disagreeing with the noxious views he expressed. But the ACLU was seeking to abide by the same neutral principles the government is obliged to follow. It is a central tenet of the First Amendment that government must be content-neutral with respect to speech.

Developing robust First Amendment law on behalf of Brandenburg was a means of promoting not only liberty but also equality, as shown by the 1982 case of *NAACP v. Claiborne Hardware*.[15] NAACP Field Secretary Charles Evers had been found liable for using intemperate language in a gathering promoting a boycott of white Mississippi merchants who

---

[14]   ACLU website, Speech on Campus, https://www.aclu.org/other/speech-campus.
[15]   NAACP v. Claiborne Hardware Co., 458 U.S. 886 (1982).

refused to support demands for equal treatment: 'If we catch any of you going in any of them racist stores, we're going to break your damn neck.' Applying the *Brandenburg* principle, the Court found that this too was protected speech because Evers's remarks, like Brandenburg's, were not intentionally, effectively, and immediately incendiary.

Civil rights hero John Lewis said that without the First Amendment, the civil rights movement would have been 'a bird without wings.'[16]

Other democracies that protect freedom of speech, like France or Germany, nevertheless ban racist or otherwise hateful speech or ban specific speech on the basis of its content, such as denial of the Holocaust. US First Amendment law does not provide for an exception to the *Brandenburg* principle for speech that is racist, antisemitic, or otherwise hateful. Some American scholars have argued that the United States should allow regulation of hate speech on the ground that there is a compelling interest in promoting equity and inclusion by protecting people who are victimized by such speech.[17] Along similar lines, Richard Delgado has argued that framing the problem of hate speech in First Amendment terms prejudges the issue, which could be considered primarily a matter of equality.[18]

But is choosing between liberty and equality a zero-sum game? Would suppression of hate speech actually promote equality or would it only abridge liberty? Opponents of hate speech exceptions to the First Amendment make a number of arguments. First, there are alternative means, other than repressing speech, to promote the important goals of inclusion and equality, as discussed below in the context of schools. Second, censoring hateful speech may be unsuccessful or even counterproductive if the ignorant or hateful views underlying the speech are not addressed and continue to fester.

---

[16]   See, e.g., Christopher M. Finan, *How Free Speech Saved Democracy: The Untold History of How the First Amendment Became an Essential Tool for Securing Liberty and Social Justice* (Lebanon, NH: Steerforth Press, 2022).

[17]   See Mari Matsuda, Public Response to Racist Speech: Considering the Victim's Story (1989) 87(8) *Michigan Law Review* 2320.

[18]   Richard Delgado, Campus Antiracism Rules: Constitutional Narratives in Collision (1990) 85 *Northwestern University Law Review* 343.

Under the First Amendment, individuals are accountable for the ideas they express. Classic First Amendment law is optimistic that exposing bad ideas in the marketplace of ideas can lead to debate and enlightenment. But optimism aside, the ultimate question is who will decide what is appropriate to say, the individual or governmental actors? *Barnette*'s clear answer is that American democracy requires siding with the individual. A third objection is a slippery slope argument. Deciding what speech is too offensive to be allowed is necessarily a subjective judgment, so allowing bans on hate speech could lead to a proliferation of censorship any time judges or school administrators find a particular expression intolerable.

A good example of the debate about the wisdom of allowing censorship of truly hateful speech is the case of *Snyder v. Phelps*.[19] Fred Phelps and followers of his Westboro Baptist Church believed that God was angry with the United States for being overly tolerant of homosexuality. Phelps drew a connection between God's anger and the death of American soldiers and picketed nearly 600 funerals brandishing signs like 'Thank God for Dead Soldiers,' attributing the fallen soldier's death to divine punishment for the government's sinful policies. The family of Marine Lance Corporal Matthew Snyder, whose funeral was picketed, brought a lawsuit against Snyder for the intentional infliction of emotional distress. An eight-Justice majority of the Supreme Court held that this obnoxious speech was nonetheless protected because it was speech on a matter of public concern.

Justice Samuel Alito wrote a solitary dissent empathizing with Snyder's family and arguing that this particular speech did not deserve First Amendment protection. The majority opinion, written by Chief Justice John Roberts, disagreed with Alito, not because the Justices valued the speech in question ('Westboro believes that America is morally flawed; many Americans might feel the same about Westboro'), and not because they did not recognize the distress of the Snyder family: '[W]e cannot react to that pain by punishing the speaker. As a Nation we have chosen a different course – to protect even hurtful speech on public issues to ensure that we do not stifle public debate.' The majority saw adhering to that principle, however painful in particular cases, as necessary to avoid

---

[19]   Snyder v. Phelps, 562 U.S. 443 (2011).

a slippery slope where government officials and judges determine what people may or may not say.

Nowhere have issues surrounding racist speech been more highly contested than on school and university campuses. During the 1980s, a number of schools and universities responded to student calls for protection against racism on campus by formulating codes prohibiting forms of offensive student conduct including speech. The University of Michigan prohibited 'any behavior, verbal or physical, that stigmatizes or victimizes an individual on the basis of race, ethnicity, religion, sex, sexual orientation, ancestry, age, marital status, handicap, or Vietnam-era veteran status.' These well-intentioned efforts to promote greater respect for vulnerable minorities on campus were not a success and may actually have been counterproductive.[20] During the few years the Michigan speech code was in effect it was invoked on multiple occasions by white students complaining that Black students had used offensive language about *their* race. Battles over who was allowed to say what – what was protected speech and what was not – exacerbated polarization.

In 1989 a federal court found the language of the Michigan code unconstitutional because it was so vague that it could stifle valuable discussion and debate about issues like race, even in the classroom.[21] It seems inevitable that hate speech codes will be vague, resulting in unpredictable and uneven applications of a provision by individual enforcers. Civil libertarians contend that better alternatives can and should be devised to include and protect vulnerable students, including education.[22]

Following the national conversation around these speech codes, many schools – even private schools that are not covered by First Amendment law – adopted policies that committed the school to policing student speech not for offensiveness but for attempts to suppress the speech of others. The 'Chicago Principles,' developed by the University of Chicago[23]

---

[20]   Samuel Walker, *Hate Speech: The History of an American Controversy* (Lincoln, NE: University of Nebraska Press, 1994).

[21]   Doe v. University of Michigan, 721 F. Supp. 852 (E.D. Mich. 1989).

[22]   Nadine Strossen, *Hate: Why We Should Resist it With Free Speech, Not Censorship* (New York: Oxford University Press, 2018).

[23]   '[D]ebate or deliberation may not be suppressed because the ideas put forth are thought by some or even by most members of the University community to be offensive, unwise, immoral, or wrong-headed. It is for the individual

and adopted by many schools around the country, articulated an active commitment to promoting free speech. The Principles also identified what was beyond the umbrella of free speech: defamation, invasions of privacy, and genuine threats or harassment could be prohibited; time, place, and manner restrictions could be imposed. Students could not be disciplined for speech someone else found offensive; students could be disciplined for using a 'heckler's veto' to drown out points of view they found offensive.

But issues about speech on campus remain far from settled. Polls show that students increasingly believe that it is possible and acceptable to make exceptions to the freedom of speech in order to insulate themselves or other students from objectionable speech or speakers. In March 2022, the Federalist Society at Yale Law School invited a conservative Christian and a liberal atheist to appear on a panel together to speak about their agreement on the politically neutral principles of free speech. The idea was that even though the panelists disagreed deeply on many issues, they nevertheless agreed that they both had the right to propound their views. Ironically, the panel was cut short by student protesters who objected to the conservative speaker appearing on campus because she had argued, in litigation and elsewhere, that religious observers should not be required to follow laws prohibiting discrimination against LGBTQ people – a view students characterized as denying the personhood of some students. The battle over this example of 'cancel culture' did not end there. Following this incident, a senior federal appellate judge, Laurence Silberman, sent an email to other federal judges suggesting that they should refuse to hire any law student who had participated in this incident. His action, in turn, was condemned as an example of the same kind of reductionist thinking he was denouncing.

---

members of the University community, not for the University as an institution, to make those judgments for themselves, and to act on those judgments not by seeking to suppress speech, but by openly and vigorously contesting the ideas that they oppose. Indeed, fostering the ability of members of the University community to engage in such debate and deliberation in an effective and responsible manner is an essential part of the University's educational mission.'

5.4   Academic freedom

Educational institutions are also a frequent venue for broader battles over the scope of the right to free expression of ideas within the classroom.

The most iconic American dispute about the scope of academic freedom, the so-called 'Monkey Trial,' involved a state's attempt to prioritize the claims of religion over academic freedom to teach science. A 1925 Tennessee state law prohibited the teaching of evolution, including the work of Charles Darwin, at any educational institution in the state. Darwinism was seen as contradicting the Bible's account of creation and was therefore objectionable to Tennesseans who did not want their children to question the Bible.

The ACLU offered to defend any teacher prosecuted under the law, and high school biology teacher John Scopes volunteered to be a test case. Scopes was prosecuted for teaching evolution and his sensational trial sparked intense national debate about the rival claims of science and religion. Scopes was represented by Clarence Darrow, an iconic trial lawyer, and Tennessee by William Jennings Bryan, a prominent national politician and Christian fundamentalist. Bryan argued simply that Scopes had violated the law; Darrow argued that religious beliefs should not be allowed to dominate public education. The presiding judge would not allow Darrow to call expert witnesses on science or education, so instead Darrow called Bryan as an expert on the Bible and subjected him to a humiliating examination about his belief in the literal truth of the biblical account that the world was created in seven days. After an eight-day trial the Tennessee jury returned a verdict of guilty in nine minutes.

The *Scopes* case never reached the Supreme Court and it did not yield any eloquent opinions about the importance of academic freedom because the state appellate court reversed the conviction on a technicality. But this highly publicized trial – in addition to 1,000 people and representatives of 100 newspapers trying to pack into the courtroom each day, the trial was the first to be covered on radio – had a major impact on public opinion. Tennessee never again attempted to enforce its law and, over the next two years, laws banning the teaching of evolution were defeated in 22 states. When a case involving an anti-evolution law finally reached the Supreme Court four decades later, in 1968, the Court unanimously declared the law unconstitutional. Seven Justices thought it was obvious that the law violated the First Amendment's Establishment Clause, which prohibits state embrace or endorsement of any religion.[24]

But, as Roger Baldwin observed, no civil liberties battle remains won. The tension between religious fundamentalism and academic freedom continued to simmer and sometimes erupt. Decades after the Court's 1968 ruling, some school districts nevertheless sought to require teachers to teach creationism alongside the teaching of evolution, as an alternative theory, so students could make a choice. In 1987, the Supreme Court ruled that requiring the teaching of creationism as a condition of teaching about evolution also violated the Establishment Clause.[25] In 2004, the Dover Pennsylvania school board adopted a requirement that the theory of 'intelligent design' be taught in conjunction with the teaching of evolution. At trial, expert witnesses described the theory of intelligent design as another incarnation of the theory of creationism, and the federal district court ruled that this requirement also violated the Establishment Clause.[26]

More recently, school boards and state legislators have attempted to regulate what students may be taught about race or sexual orientation. Between 2020 and 2022, more than a dozen states adopted vague bans on teaching 'critical race theory,' or otherwise limiting how race may be taught, and similar legislation was introduced in other states. Critical race theory is a legal doctrine contending that the structures of law are infused with racism, and so racism is systemic rather than being attributable only to individual bigots. This observation is undeniably correct. Examples of laws that perpetuate racism include criminal laws promoting mass incarceration, and superficially neutral education or housing laws that exacerbate previous inequities.[27] But the term 'critical race theory' came to be used as a shorthand for teaching about racism in any way that might make

---

[24] Epperson v. Arkansas, 393 U.S. 97 (1968).

[25] Edwards v. Aguillard, 482 U.S. 578 (1987).

[26] Kitzmiller v. Dover Area School District, 400 F. Supp. 2d 707 (M.D. Pa. 2005).

[27] The GI Bill offering low-cost mortgages to World War II veterans, for example, did not by its terms exclude non-white veterans, but the program was structured in a way that made benefits unavailable to people who were unable to meet its conditions due to local segregation and racist practices. It is estimated that a million Black veterans were denied the opportunity to capitalize on this benefit. Legal and financial advantages based on home ownership continue to disproportionately disadvantage Black families.

white children feel uncomfortable, and became a catch-all phrase often sweeping in diversity and inclusion efforts as well as education about race and racism. A 2021 Oklahoma law, for example, prohibited teaching the history of white supremacy or the concept of 'white privilege.'[28] Some legislators would have gone even further, prohibiting teaching that 'one race is the unique oppressor in the institution of slavery' and 'another race is the unique victim in the institution of slavery.'[29]

Proponents of these laws argued that 'critical race theory' is divisive, that children should not be made to feel guilty about their race, and that presenting children with negative views of American history will discourage them from being patriotic. Opponents saw these bills as backlash to recent calls for enhancing diversity and inclusion in education and in standard accounts of American history, which tend to ignore or minimize the horrors of slavery, lynching, segregation, and vicious attempts to keep Black people from voting.

The first constitutional challenge to one of these laws came in Oklahoma. The lawsuit argued that the Oklahoma law was so vague that it could not only silence criticism of a whitewashed view of history, but lead to important aspects of American history and critical issues about race relations not being discussed in classrooms at all. Oklahoma teachers were faced with an impossible and unconstitutional choice: avoid topics related to race or open themselves to criticism and risk losing their teaching licenses. While teachers should teach about such painful matters with sensitivity, it would be a repudiation of classic First Amendment principles to uphold these vague, repressive laws. If learning about American history is divisive and guilt-inducing, that is because of the racial divides in American history itself.

---

[28]   Educators may not teach that 'individuals, by virtue of sex, race, ethnicity, religion, color, or national origin, are inherently responsible for actions committed in the past by other members of the same sex, race, ethnicity, religion, color, or national origin.' '[No] individual should feel discomfort, guilt, anguish or any other form of psychological distress on account of his or her race or sex.'

[29]   Ben Felder, As Critical Race Theory Stirs National Debate, Oklahoma Bill Seeks to Alter Teaching of Slavery (*The Oklahoman*, December 16, 2021) https://www.oklahoman.com/story/news/2021/12/16/critical-race-theory -oklahoma-rep-jim-olsen-bill-teaching-slavery/8912667002/.

In 2022, the state of Florida adopted a law wholly forbidding instruction on sexual orientation and gender identity in kindergarten through third grade. Opponents argue that the 'Don't Say Gay' law, as it was dubbed, would marginalize LGBTQ people, preventing a teacher, for example, from explaining the fact that a student has two parents of the same sex. As in the 'critical race theory' bans, examples of a few teachers discussing controversial subject matter in a manner inappropriate to the age of their students were taken to justify a content-based restriction on all speech on a particular subject.

This recent wave of repression shows again that free speech and equality are not diametrically opposed goals. Discussion of America's racialized history and of students' families is far more likely to promote understanding than is censorship. The examples provided also show that the bedrock First Amendment idea of neutral principles is under siege from more than one direction.

5.5   Students' rights

Another battleground in the war over speech on campus is the issue of what political and other viewpoints students can express without fear of reprisal.

The Supreme Court first announced that neither students nor teachers 'shed their constitutional rights to freedom of speech or expression at the schoolhouse gate' in the case of *Tinker v. Des Moines Independent Community School District* (1969).[30] Thirteen-year-old Mary Beth Tinker, along with her brother and a few friends, decided to wear black armbands to school as a symbolic protest to express support for a truce in the Vietnam war. In response to the students' campaign the school adopted a policy, later affirmed by the school district, that students who refused to remove their armbands in school could be suspended. This policy was presented as being necessary to avoid disruption and disorder in the school.

---

[30]   Tinker v. Des Moines Independent Community School District, 393 U.S. 503 (1969).

Although the lower courts had ruled against Tinker, a seven Justice supermajority of the Supreme Court ruled that the school did not have sufficient reason to prohibit students from peacefully wearing armbands. To justify the suppression of the students' expression of their political beliefs, the Court said, the school officials must be able to show that the conduct in question would 'materially and substantially interfere' with the operation of the school – the same kind of high standard as *Brandenburg*. In this case, although the school district feared possible disruption, the administrators were unable to point to any actual problem. As Justice Louis Brandeis once observed, '[t]he greatest dangers to liberty lurk in insidious encroachment by men of zeal, well-meaning but without understanding.'[31]

The *Tinker* standard, which gives the courts a veto over public school policy suppressing or punishing speech, was applied in the more recent and less political case of *Mahanoy Area School District v. B.L.* (2021).[32] Brandi Levy, not identified by her full name in the case because she was a minor, was upset when she tried out for cheerleader and made only the junior varsity squad. She posted a photograph of herself on Snapchat with the caption, 'Fuck school fuck softball fuck cheer fuck everything.' The coaches decided that this post violated school and team rules and punished Levy by suspending her from the squad.

A supermajority of the Court (eight Justices) ruled that this action violated Levy's First Amendment rights. The Court summarized its previous case law which, in addition to allowing schools to regulate conduct that is actually disruptive, had found that schools may regulate student speech in three circumstances: (1) indecent, lewd, or vulgar speech on school grounds; (2) speech promoting illicit drug use during a class trip; and (3) speech that others may reasonably perceive as 'bear[ing] the imprimatur of the school, such as that appearing in a school-sponsored newspaper.' The Court found that although schools might under different circumstances be permitted to regulate speech beyond school grounds, as a general matter supervision of off-campus speech is a job for parents, not for the school.

---

[31]   Olmstead v. United States, 277 U.S. 438 (1928) (dissenting opinion).
[32]   Mahanoy Area School District v. B.L., 594 U.S. ___ (2021).

The Court did not distinguish *Tinker* on the basis that Levy's outburst was not valuable political speech. 'It might be tempting to dismiss B.L'.s words as unworthy of the robust First Amendment protections discussed herein,' Justice Stephen Breyer wrote in his short majority opinion. 'But sometimes it is necessary to protect the superfluous in order to preserve the necessary.'

5.6   Campaign finance

Campaign finance regulation is one of the most controversial areas of the Supreme Court's free speech jurisprudence, where some critics see the Court as having unduly prioritized free speech over equal democratic participation.

In the 1976 case of *Buckley v. Valeo*,[33] the Court reviewed provisions of a federal law seeking to limit the influence of money on elections. When Senator James Buckley challenged the constitutionality of the law, the Court struck down the statute's limitation on campaign expenditures as an abridgment of speech, on the theory that the expenditure of money in campaigns, especially the money spent by candidates, directly or indirectly supports the expression of political views. 'Discussion of public issues and debate on the qualifications of candidates are integral to the operation of the system of government established by our Constitution. The First Amendment affords the broadest protection to such political expression.'

On the other hand, the Court upheld the statute's limits on campaign contributions – $1,000 on individual contributions to a single candidate; $5,000 limit for political action committee contributions to a single candidate; and a $25,000 limitation on all individual contributions in one year – reasoning that the government has a compelling interest in preventing corruption or its appearance, an interest that is well served by avoiding the appearance or actuality of campaign donors owning a candidate.[34] In subsequent decades, the Court continued to observe the distinction

---

[33]   Buckley v. Valeo, 424 U.S. 1 (1976).
[34]   The Court also upheld the statute's requirement of disclosure of all campaign contributions, but with a safe harbor for small, controversial parties

between contributions and expenditures. Later cases upheld campaign contribution limits unless they were deemed unreasonably low, but recent case law may have planted the seed for striking down more campaign contribution limitations in the future.[35]

Although earlier cases had allowed limitations on corporate spending in political campaigns, the notorious *Citizens United* case[36] reversed those rulings. A law that prohibited corporations, unions, and even non-profit organizations like the ACLU from using their general treasury funds for express advocacy or electioneering communications was found to be a violation of First Amendment speech rights.

Critics have ardently condemned the Court's equation of money with speech in *Buckley* as well as the protection of corporate spending in *Citizens United*. Because money, especially corporate money, has such a distorting influence on politics, they contend, adopting a libertarian free speech position is undemocratic, minimizing the clout of less affluent Americans. The strength of that argument depends on what one sees as the purposes of the First Amendment. If a central goal of the First Amendment is to promote equal participation in democracy, laws leveling the playing field can be viewed as consistent with that egalitarian goal. If on the other hand, the overarching goal is to limit the government's ability to repress speech, then the libertarian result in *Buckley* becomes more attractive.[37] Giving government the power to regulate expenditures in campaigns creates a risk of partisan enforcement, harking back to the discriminatory enforcement of the early sedition law described in Section 3.1.

The ruling of *Citizens United* is non-partisan, allowing corporations of any political valence to spend money to influence political debate. If those policies fall unequally in practice, it is due to the underlying inequality in American society. Should it be the role of the Court, wielding the First

---

like the Socialist Workers Party. The extent of required disclosure has also been a fraught issue.

[35]   In McCutcheon v. FEC, 572 U.S. 185 (2015), the Court invalidated aggregate limits on annual contributions by individuals, overruling the contrary holding in *Buckley*.

[36]   Citizens United v. Federal Election Commission, 558 U.S. 310 (2010).

[37]   Joel M. Gora, Free Speech Matters: The Roberts Court and the First Amendment (2016) 25(1) *Journal of Law and Policy*.

Amendment, to try to reduce the impact of that inequality on politics or should content neutrality be treated as a categorical imperative?

Regulation of campaign finance is likely to remain controversial. Realizing that the current Court is unlikely to overrule *Buckley* or *Citizens United*, supporters of tighter campaign finance regulation have called for a constitutional amendment. Others, including the ACLU, contend that the best solution to the very real problem of money in politics is public financing of elections, which is politically challenging to effect but consistent with most people's views of First Amendment jurisprudence, including the Supreme Court's.

5.7   The scope of First Amendment 'speech'

The First Amendment guarantee of free speech can aptly be denominated as freedom of expression, as the 'speech' covered has been interpreted to include symbolic speech and other forms of expressive conduct, from burning a flag or a draft card as a form of protest, to choice of attire, to nude dancing in a strip club.[38]

It is settled law that an individual's right to free expression may be limited by appropriate time, place, and manner restrictions. Although people cannot be prohibited from expressing an unpopular idea, they can be prohibited from expressing any idea with a bullhorn in a residential neighborhood in the middle of the night. Anti-abortion demonstrators may not be prohibited from picketing abortion clinics, but they may be required to keep their distance from the clinic entrance or from individual visitors.

Not all forms of speech or expression, however, enjoy the solicitous protection of the speech in *Barnette*, *Tinker*, and *Mahanoy*. In a number of contexts the Supreme Court has ruled that particular forms of expression should not receive First Amendment protection at all, or should receive a milder form of judicial review. This categorical approach, which has

---

[38]   Mark Tushnet's *Advanced Introduction to Free Expression* (Cheltenham, UK: Edward Elgar, 2018) provides a very useful study of the structure of legal doctrine governing free expression, identifying and discussing paradigms underlying the law discussed here.

been criticized,[39] has been applied to exclude 'fighting words' and obscenity from any First Amendment protection.

The fighting words doctrine originated in a 1942 case, *Chaplinsky v. New Hampshire*,[40] involving a Jehovah's Witness who publicly called the town marshal 'a God-damned racketeer' and 'a damned Fascist.' The Court ruled that Chaplinsky's personally insulting words were not protected by the First Amendment. Some of the Court's explanation for its ruling in that case is in tension with the later and more rigorous *Brandenburg* test and, perhaps for that reason, the doctrine has not been applied recently. But *Chaplinsky* has not explicitly been reversed and so the fighting words exception remains in lists of types of speech not covered by the First Amendment.

The Court has never retreated from its decision to treat obscenity as beyond the scope of the First Amendment.[41] In what is obviously a highly subjective test, the Court defines obscenity as speech or expression which appeals to prurient interest because of its patently offensive sexual content and which lacks any serious social value. In one obscenity case, Justice Potter Stewart famously remarked that although he regarded it as impossible to clearly define what constitutes obscenity, 'I know it when I see it.'[42] The Court's categorical approach, simply excluding what it regards as obscene from any First Amendment protection, has been heavily criticized. Dismissing everything deemed obscene as unworthy of any constitutional protection preempts the question of whether the state actually has any legitimate interest in regulating sexually explicit publications or conduct. Exactly what is the harm that obscenity causes? Should morality be considered a sufficient justification for overriding individual choice of reading or viewing material?[43] And what is the cost of allowing this form of government censorship?

---

39   Frederick Schauer, Categories and the First Amendment: A Play in Three Acts (1981) 34(2) *Vanderbilt Law Review* 265.
40   Chaplinsky v. New Hampshire, 315 U.S. 568 (1942).
41   Roth v. United States, 354 U.S. 476 (1957); Paris Adult Theatre I v. Slaton, 413 U.S. 49 (1973).
42   Jacobellis v. Ohio, 378 U.S. 184 (1964) (concurring opinion).
43   Harry Kalven, The Metaphysics of the Law of Obscenity (1960) 1 *The Supreme Court Review*.

Unlike hard-core obscenity, pornography is deemed to be within the ambit of the First Amendment and so government regulation of pornography is likely to be struck down on the ground that the individual rather than the government should get to decide what to write, produce, read, or view. But, as in the area of hate speech, arguments have been made that regulation of pornography would serve important purposes beyond claims of morality. Catharine MacKinnon and Andrea Dworkin have argued that regulation would protect the civil rights of women, who are objectified and degraded by pornography.[44] MacKinnon and Dworkin drafted a model ordinance defining illegal pornography as the graphic sexually explicit subordination of women, whether in pictures or in words. When the City of Indianapolis adopted such an ordinance, the Seventh Circuit Court of Appeals[45] found that it was unconstitutional because it attempted to regulate speech based on its content: portrayals of women. Obscenity law was said to be distinguishable because that doctrine devalues speech based not on its content but on its inherent nature of appealing to prurient interests. Courts might also have found the anti-pornography ordinance vague.

One source of contention has been whether, as an empirical matter, regulation would serve an additional interest on the theory that pornography can lead to physical harm by encouraging hostile attitudes to women and increasing the propensity to commit or condone sexual assault. Without actual proof of such a connection, the First Amendment freedom prevails over speculative concerns, as it did in *Tinker*.

Not all feminists agree that pornography should be subject to regulation. Former ACLU president Nadine Strossen has argued that women's rights and equality are more threatened by censorship than by sexual words or images, as censorship has been used to suppress information about women's equality, health, and reproductive freedom.[46] Strossen disagrees that First Amendment freedom with respect to pornography clashes with

---

44   Catharine MacKinnon, *Toward A Feminist Theory of The State* (Cambridge, MA: Harvard University Press, 1989); Catharine MacKinnon, Pornography, Civil Rights and Speech (1985) 20(1) *Harvard Civil Rights-Civil Liberties Law Review*.

45   American Booksellers Association, Inc. v. Hudnut, 771 F.2d 323 (7th Cir. 1985).

46   Nadine Strossen, *Defending Pornography: Free Speech and the Fight for Women's Rights* (New York: Scribner, 1995).

equality interests, arguing that free speech in this context too can promote equality.

5.8   Categories of less protected speech

The Supreme Court has delineated other categories of speech which, while not wholly excluded from First Amendment protection, receive less stringent levels of judicial review than political speech.

For years, commercial speech, typified by advertising, was regarded as categorically beyond the First Amendment's protection. Commercial speech, it was thought, added little of relevance to the political process. In 1976, the Court reversed course, deciding that commercial advertising should be considered a form of speech protected by the First Amendment.[47] But subsequent cases established that commercial speech would not receive the same kind of protection as other forms of speech. Some observers thought the Court's decision to end the categorical exclusion was sound because it is difficult to explain why commercial speech is not speech. Is there a real distinction based on the economic motivation or the commercial subject matter? Others more cynically saw the Court as siding with business interests.

The jurisprudence in the commercial speech area has been confused and confusing ever since. What is clear is that the multi-factor test the Court now applies to government regulation of commercial speech[48] – to protect the public against fraud, for example – allows the Court to veto policy decisions government used to make without judicial review, in service of a libertarian view of the value of speech, just as it can in political speech cases.

Another analytical dichotomy the Court has generated that determines how much leeway a governmental entity has to regulate expression is

---

[47]   Virginia Board of Pharmacy v. Virginia Citizens Consumer Council, 425 U.S. 748 (1976).

[48]   The test is derived from Central Hudson Gas & Electric Corporation v. Public Service Commission of New York, 447 U.S. 557 (1980).

the public forum doctrine. The idea here, traceable to a 1939 decision,[49] is that if an area owned by a governmental unit has become a forum for public exchange of views, government may not exclude some but not other speakers on the basis of the content of their speech. This idea can apply to public streets or gathering places, or to public university arenas designed for and dedicated to expressive activities. In non-public forums, the public owner of the space may 'reserve the forum for its intended purposes, communicative or otherwise, as long as the regulation on speech is reasonable and not an effort to suppress expression merely because public officials oppose the speaker's view.'[50] The non-public forum category has, for example, included a military installation, which is allowed to exclude all speakers who want to express a viewpoint – like picketers – as long as the military does not discriminate among picketers depending on the viewpoint they wish to express.

In an interesting recent application of the public forum doctrine, the Second Circuit Court of Appeals found that President Donald Trump created a public forum on Twitter, @realDonaldTrump, by his use of a social media platform for public discussion, and therefore could not deny access to particular people who criticized him or his presidency. '[T]he First Amendment does not permit a public official who utilizes a social media account for all manner of official purposes to exclude persons from an otherwise-open online dialogue because they expressed views with which the official disagrees.'[51] The litigation continued when Trump continued to exclude certain participants, but mooted out when Trump was no longer president – without the Supreme Court having expressed its view.

5.9   Current issues concerning free speech

New First Amendment issues continue to arise as new technologies emerge.

---

[49]   Hague v. Committee for Industrial Organization, 307 U.S. 496 (1939).
[50]   Perry Education Association v. Perry Local Educators' Association, 460 U.S. 37 (1983).
[51]   Knight First Amendment Institute v. Trump, 928 F.3d 226 (2d Cir. 2019).

Even the most ardent originalists do not doubt that the First Amendment applies to the Internet.[52] But many people contend that the world of social media poses distinct challenges to received First Amendment doctrine.[53] Existing doctrine establishes that because the First Amendment applies to governmental action, the government may not constitutionally police the Internet or social media, or regulate social media companies either by requiring them to monitor and remove speech or preventing them from doing so. On the other hand, social media companies, as private entities, do not violate the First Amendment by deciding to allow or prohibit particular speech.

But should these new marketplaces of ideas be subject to greater limitation than traditional forms of speech in order to counter the rapid proliferation of falsehoods and inflammatory conspiracy theories? And what First Amendment paradigm best applies in this new context? Do social media companies have their own First Amendment rights as speakers or news editors? Are they providers of digital public forums?[54] Do they exercise a government-like power in moderating user content? If the controlling rationale for free speech is a libertarian idea that all individuals have the right to decide on the content and form of their speech, should First Amendment principles be extended to disallow powerful social media companies from banishing people from their forums – a challenge to the traditional public/private distinction? If faith in a free marketplace of ideas has been based on the hopeful assumption that open debate helps truth to prevail, is that assumption still valid in a marketplace subject to massive influxes of false speech under conditions of unequal access? As in the campaign finance area, should securing democracy and equalizing disparate power to speak be treated as goals shaping First Amendment doctrine?

Congress put a thumb on the scale of this debate in Section 230 of the Communications Decency Act, giving social media companies, along with Internet services providers, immunity from lawsuits brought on

---

52   Reno v. ACLU, 521 U.S. 844 (1997), for example, voided provisions of a Communications Decency Act aimed at shielding minors from 'indecency.'
53   Richard L. Hasen, *Cheap Speech* (New Haven, CT: Yale University Press, 2022).
54   Valerie C. Brannon, *Free Speech and the Regulation of Social Media Content* (Washington, DC: Congressional Research Service, 2019).

the basis of the false or inflammatory nature of material their users have posted.[55] This immunity removes an incentive for the companies to take down controversial posts, thus promoting freedom of speech, for better or worse, in these popular forums. Whether or not Congress should repeal that immunity is one of the many areas of controversy surrounding social media.

---

[55]   'No provider or user of an interactive computer service shall be treated as the publisher or speaker of any information provided by another information content provider.'

6　Other First Amendment freedoms

6.1　Freedom of assembly

Freedom of assembly, also covered in the First Amendment, is intimately related to freedom of speech as well as the right to petition for redress of grievances. The ability to form associations and to demonstrate publicly amplifies the voice of individuals and the likelihood that their viewpoint will be heard. The civil rights era was defined by iconic marches; large demonstrations opposed the Iraq War in 2003; women wearing pink pussy hats reacted to the election of Donald Trump in 2017; massive protests against police misconduct followed the murder of George Floyd in 2020.

But this right too had to be won in the courts. In the early twentieth century, the same forces that wanted to limit individual speech regarded as threatening also wanted to control or prevent groups of people from assembling or marching to promote their fighting faiths. *Hague v. CIO*,[1] for example, concerned an attempt to suppress labor organizing. In that case, the Court upheld the right to peaceful assembly on a public forum rationale, despite the controversial nature of the message:

> Wherever the title of street and parks may rest, they have immemorately been held in trust for the use of the public and time out of mind, have been used for purposes of assembly, communicating thoughts between citizens, and discussing public questions. Such use of the streets and public places has from ancient times, been a part of the privileges, immunities, rights, and liberties of citizens.

---

[1]　Hague v. Committee for Industrial Organization, 307 U.S. 496 (1939).

Early ACLU leaders challenged laws prohibiting assembly without a permit, with leaders sometimes inviting arrest by dramatically reading the words of the First Amendment to illegally gathered crowds, in at least one instance while photogenically standing on top of a car.

The civil rights movement of the 1960s revived the battles of the 1920s and 1930s when advocates took to the streets and law enforcement officials tried to shut down their demonstrations through physical force or the force of law. *Cox v. Louisiana*[2] arose when several thousand demonstrators protesting the arrest of civil rights advocates marched through Baton Rouge, Louisiana, ending their peaceful march in front of the local courthouse. The Chief of Police initially told Cox, a leader of the group, that the demonstrators could stay in a designated area, but later told them to leave and then used tear gas to disperse the crowd. The next day, Cox was arrested for 'disturbing the peace,' 'obstructing public passages,' and 'intent of interfering with … the administration of justice.' The Louisiana courts upheld his conviction, but the US Supreme Court reversed, finding that the applicable state law violated the First Amendment rights of speech and assembly because it was too vague and thus allowed too much discretion to those enforcing it. The statute, for example, prohibited demonstrating 'near' a courthouse with the intention of influencing the judicial system. The Chief of Police had first told Cox that his group was not too 'near' the courthouse, but then changed his mind.

Cox and other cases established that the right of assembly is subject to reasonable time, place, and manner regulation in light of conflicting demands for the use of public places like parks and sidewalks. But it cannot be subject to authorities' approval or disapproval of the demonstrators' point of view.

That proposition was tested when a group of neo-Nazis announced their intention of holding a demonstration in Skokie, Illinois in 1977. Skokie was home to a number of Jewish Holocaust survivors, and the city decided to try to protect their sensibilities by taking measures, including going to court and seeking an injunction, to keep the Nazis from demonstrating. The city's lawyers understood that the approach of seeking a prior restraint on speech and assembly had been disfavored by the Supreme Court in the civil rights cases of the 1960s, and advised that if the group

---

[2]   Cox v. Louisiana, 379 U.S. 536 (1965).

were to hold their planned assembly, it would soon be forgotten. But the city went ahead with its litigation and won a preliminary injunction.

History has distorted and sensationalized what the Nazis actually planned to do. The idea that the Nazis intended to march through Skokie came from a misstatement of the facts in the judicial opinion granting the city's injunction, a sign of the judge's reaction to the emotional threat of the presence of Nazis in Skokie. The group did not plan to march through residential areas, but to have 25 to 50 people picket in front of the Skokie City Hall for about 30 minutes, holding placards that said 'Free Speech for White People' to protest the fact that they had been denied permission to demonstrate in Chicago area parks.[3] Ultimately, the courts ruled that the First Amendment protected the right of the group, whatever their beliefs, to express their views in a peaceful demonstration. And then, having provoked considerable attention and threats of violent counter-demonstrations, the Nazis decided not to go to Skokie after all, as long as they were permitted to demonstrate in Chicago public parks.

Echoes of Skokie sounded in 2017 when the City of Charlottesville, Virginia, revoked a permit it had granted to a white supremacist group that planned a demonstration to protest the removal of a Robert E. Lee confederate statue from a local park. The ACLU of Virginia agreed to represent the organizers, who asserted that their demonstration would be peaceful – a condition of the First Amendment right of assembly. As in Skokie, the organization was criticized for representing hateful speakers, but adhered to the ideal of content neutrality. If Charlottesville were allowed to censor the speech of white supremacists on the ground that their speech was likely to provoke strong reactions, what would stop any city from denying permits to a group like Black Lives Matter, whose views inflame different segments of the population? The Charlottesville demonstration turned violent, leading to soul-searching within the ACLU as well as in the media about whether the violence was foreseeable, and how the organization could best serve the interests of both equality and liberty.

Starting in 2017, state legislators introduced a wave of bills designed to constrain and deter demonstrations: sharply increasing criminal penalties for common tactics like blocking traffic and tearing down monuments;

---

[3]   Philippa Strum, *When the Nazis Came to Skokie: Freedom for the Speech We Hate* (Lawrence, KA: University Press of Kansas, 1999).

and attempting to squelch indigenous people's environmental demonstrations by reclassifying oil pipelines as critical infrastructure. Following the 2020 surge of Black Lives Matter protests inspired by the murder of George Floyd (see Section 8.5), the wave became a tsunami, with somewhere around 100 bills proposed to expand criminal liability for conduct during a demonstration and even to strip governmental benefits – including pandemic relief – from anyone convicted of a demonstration-related offense. Most, but not all, of these extreme bills were defeated. States also sought to hold demonstration organizers liable for unanticipated harm caused by another demonstrator,[4] and to immunize drivers whose cars hit protesters. Black Lives Matter demonstrators were subjected to repressive policing, including arbitrary arrests and use of tear gas. When so many American legislators and law enforcement officers once again regard expression of views they dislike as justifying a forceful response, the channels of democracy are threatened.[5] No civil liberty remains won.

Freedom of association, like freedom of speech, has been claimed as a counterweight to anti-discrimination law, sometimes successfully. The Supreme Court found, for example, that the Boy Scouts of America had the right to revoke the membership of James Dale when they discovered that he was gay.[6] A lower court had found that the compelling interest in preventing discrimination outweighed the Boy Scouts' associational freedom, but a five-Justice majority in the Supreme Court found that forcing the Boy Scouts to include Dale would significantly affect the organization's right of expressive association. On the other hand, claims of landlords and employers that they have a constitutional right to disregard fair housing or employment laws on the basis of their freedom of association have not been successful, so far.

---

[4]   See Mckesson v. Doe, 592 U.S. ___ (2020), part of the lengthy litigation over whether Black Lives Matter organizer Delray Mckesson could be held liable under Louisiana law for another demonstrator's throwing an object that hit a police officer.

[5]   In 2013, INCLO issued a report called *Take Back the Streets*, documenting the worldwide crackdown on dissent.

[6]   Boy Scouts of America v. Dale, 530 U.S. 640 (2000).

6.2   Freedom of the press

Freedom of the press, also included in the First Amendment, was an incendiary issue for the colonists before the American Revolution. Libel laws were used as a means of suppressing the colonists' criticisms of the actions of the king and colonial government – the kinds of criticisms that found their way into the Declaration of Independence.

The colonists fought back. In the most notorious case of that era, printer John Peter Zenger was sued for libel for printing articles in the *New York Weekly Journal* in 1733 accusing the royal governor of New York, William Cosby, of corruption. The anonymous article asserted that Cosby had rigged elections, allowed the French enemy to scout New York harbor, and had intended to enslave New Yorkers. It did not legally matter whether or not these assertions were true. Under English law at the time, truth was not a defense in this type of libel action as libel simply consisted of opposing the government. And it did not matter that Zenger had not written the pieces in question but had only printed them. Zenger was pressured to identify the anonymous authors, but steadfastly refused to do so even when he was jailed for a year.

At his 1735 trial, Zenger's lawyer, Andrew Hamilton, admitted that Zenger had printed the pieces in question. Since that eliminated Zenger's only available legal defense, the judge directed the jury to find in favor of Cosby. But Hamilton had pleaded with the jury to help to uphold freedom of the press despite the law. 'It is not the cause of one poor printer,' he argued, 'but the cause of liberty.'[7] The jury took only ten minutes to nullify the law and find in favor of Zenger.

When freedom of the press was included in the First Amendment, the primary goal was to empower the press to serve as a check on government in order to prevent abusive use of power – as in Zenger's case.[8]

---

[7]   James Alexander and Stanley N. Katz (eds), *A Brief Narrative on the Case and Trial of John Peter Zenger, Printer of the New York Weekly Journal* (Cambridge, MA: Belknap, 1963).

[8]   Vincent Blasi, The Checking Value in First Amendment Theory (1977) 2(3) *American Bar Foundation Research Journal* 521.

Zenger would be glad to know that the Supreme Court to date has interpreted the First Amendment as providing the press with substantial protection against broad libel laws. The landmark case of *New York Times v. Sullivan* (1964) was litigated against the backdrop of the civil rights movement.[9] The *Times* had printed an advertisement sponsored by civil rights activists seeking contributions to a voting rights campaign, to support the student movement, and to help defend Dr. Martin Luther King against pending charges. The advertisement, entitled 'Heed Their Rising Voices,' asserted that peaceful protests in Montgomery had been met with a 'wave of terror,' and gave examples of violent and excessive conduct of 'Southern violators' including police. Most of the statements were accurate, but some details – like the number of times King had been arrested and the song demonstrators had been singing on a particular occasion – were incorrect. J.T. Sullivan, Montgomery's City Commissioner in charge of the police, brought a libel action under Alabama law against the *New York Times* and four Black clergymen who had signed the advertisement. He claimed that readers would associate him with some of the advertisement's allegations against the police. Although he had not shown that he had suffered any harm, an Alabama jury awarded him $500,000 in damages, the full amount he had requested.

The Supreme Court unanimously ruled that the fact that some of the contested assertions were untrue was not a sufficient basis for the libel verdict. The First Amendment, said the Court, requires that the plaintiff in a libel or defamation action show that the defendant actually knew that a statement regarding matters of public interest was false, or was reckless in deciding to publish the information without investigating whether it was accurate – an 'actual malice' standard. Justice William Brennan analogized the Alabama libel laws to the notorious Sedition Act of 1798, which he described as having crystallized a national awareness of the central meaning of the First Amendment. He wrote of our

> profound national commitment to the principle that debate on public issues should be uninhibited, robust, and wide-open, and that it may well include vehement, caustic, and sometimes unpleasantly sharp attacks on government and public officials ... The present advertisement, as an expression of grievance and protest on one of the major public issues of our time, would seem clearly to qualify for the constitutional protection. The question is whether it

---

[9]   New York Times v. Sullivan, 376 U.S. 254 (1964).

forfeits that protection by the falsity of some of its factual statements and by its alleged defamation of respondent.[10]

A truth defense was not considered sufficient protection for the press. '[E]rroneous statement is inevitable in free debate, and … must be protected if the freedoms of expression are to have the breathing space that they need … to survive.' The Court subsequently extended the high 'actual malice' standard for prevailing in a libel or defamation action to all 'public figures,' not just public officials, making it difficult for anyone considered a public figure to win a libel action.[11] The future of this standard may be uncertain. Recently, several Supreme Court Justices have questioned whether the actual malice standard is too high and whether *New York Times v. Sullivan* should be overruled.[12]

Another issue central to freedom of the press is whether or not government can prevent publication of allegedly dangerous materials – prior restraint of publication.[13] In the World War I sedition cases, the people who spoke out were prosecuted after they had already conveyed their views. The Supreme Court in 1931 endorsed the principle that even if the press might be held accountable after the fact for publishing material in violation of a law, government should only rarely be allowed to gag the press by preventing publication. The state law at issue in that case[14] allowed officials to seek an injunction against publication of a 'malicious, scandalous and defamatory newspaper,' which had alleged that government officials were protecting gangsters and called for a grand jury inquiry.

Unlike the libel law defense set out in *New York Times v. Sullivan*, the ban on prior restraint had a lengthy historical pedigree, tracing back to English law. As the 1931 Court said, 'the liberty of the press, historically considered and taken up by the Federal Constitution, has meant,

---

[10]   Ibid.
[11]   Ibid.
[12]   Berisha v. Lawson, 141 S. Ct. 2424 (2021) (Justices Thomas and Gorsuch dissenting from denial of *certiorari*).
[13]   Leonard Levy, *The Emergence of a Free Press* (New York: Oxford University Press, 1985) (identifying freedom from prior restraint as central to what the framers intended in the First Amendment provision, and challenging other received ideas about what the amendment was intended to cover).
[14]   Near v. Minnesota, 283 U.S. 697 (1931).

principally, although not exclusively, immunity from previous restraints or censorship.' After invoking eighteenth-century English law scholar William Blackstone, the Court quoted James Madison as saying of the guarantee of a free press, 'it is better to leave a few of its noxious branches to their luxuriant growth than, by pruning them away, to injure the vigour of those yielding the proper fruits.' The Court set out a few exceptional circumstances where the governmental interest might be strong enough to outweigh the general presumption against prior restraint: preventing exposure of sensitive information about troop movements, or obscenity.

Decades later, in another landmark case, the Nixon Administration sought to enjoin the *New York Times* from publishing the 'History of US Decision-Making in Vietnam, 1945–68,' a study of the Vietnam War colloquially known as the 'Pentagon Papers.' Even during the Civil War and World Wars I and II no administration had attempted to censor newspapers by preventing them from publishing information. The papers in this 7,000-page history, classified by the government as secret, had been given to the newspapers by a whistleblower, Daniel Ellsberg, who secretly copied the material. Ellsberg, who had initially supported the war, thought that if the American people knew the whole story of US involvement in Vietnam, they would be converted, as he had been.

After the *Times* had published two installments of the papers, the Nixon Administration sought a restraining order against further publication on the ground that release of these confidential papers could damage national security. Ellsberg then also gave a copy of the Pentagon Papers to the *Washington Post*, which resulted in a second lawsuit over the *Post*'s prospective publication. Both of the district judges involved denied the administration's request for a restraining order, but the two Courts of Appeals reached opposite results on appeal, with the Second Circuit Court of Appeals in New York agreeing to issue a restraining order.

Because the presses were on hold pending the outcome of the litigation, the Supreme Court held oral arguments the very next day after agreeing to hear the case – a truly remarkable timetable. The Court then issued its decision only four days after argument.[15] Probably because there was not sufficient time to hammer out a consensus, the six-Justice majority contented itself with issuing a brief, *per curiam* (unsigned) opinion over-

---

[15]   New York Times Co. v. United States, 403 U.S. 713 (1971).

turning the restraining order and allowing publication. And in separate concurring opinions, the six Justices each offered their own explanations of why they thought the government had failed to meet the heavy burden of justifying a prior restraint on publication. Some of the Justices invoked lofty principles about the need for a free press; others thought the president had overstepped the authority granted him by Congress.

On the whole, the Pentagon Papers case was more a landmark in its notoriety than in the development of a robust law of freedom of the press. The splintered opinions left unclear whether or not the newspapers could be charged with a crime under the espionage laws after the fact, based on their publication of classified material – as two Justices explicitly said they thought would be permissible. And the case did not establish rights for whistleblowers, or for the public to gain access to information about government activity. Justice William Douglas later noted that although the Pentagon Papers case is celebrated for curtailing government censorship, the government had actually succeeded in suppressing publication for two weeks, an unprecedented victory for censorship.[16] Now, with the advent of the Internet, a whistleblower would no longer have to wait for printing presses to roll, but could immediately publish material. And so the Court's prohibition of prior restraint now seems less consequential than its failure to address the rights of whistleblowers, the right of the public to know what the government is doing, or the constitutional validity of the Espionage Act.

There is no need to prevent the press from publishing the government's secrets if the press is unable to ferret out those secrets in the first place. While the World War I Sedition Act was repealed after the war, the Espionage Act was not. Between 1919 and 2007, only one person was prosecuted for violating the Espionage Act by revealing government secrets. But the Obama Administration, citing the need for zero tolerance of leaks, used the Espionage Act on multiple occasions to prosecute a series of whistleblowers including Edward Snowden and Chelsea Manning. The Trump Administration continued to crack down on potential whistleblowers as well as journalists to try to prevent the government's secrets from being exposed.

---

16   David Rudenstine, *The Day the Presses Stopped: A History of the Pentagon Papers Case* (Berkeley, CA: University of California Press, 1998).

US journalists have not suffered the degree of blatant censorship of the press or official attacks on journalists prevalent in authoritarian countries. The courts and public opinion have served as a buffer. But threats to journalists from individuals and officials have increased in recent years. President Donald Trump expressed considerable intolerance for a free press, regularly deriding individual journalists and media, claiming the right to exclude reporters he regarded as hostile from press conferences, demanding journalists' confidential records, and advocating relaxation of libel laws so that he could sue reporters who criticized him. It is dangerous to fan hostility to journalists who express opposing political viewpoints rather than accepting the fact that in a free society members of the press will tell stories differently. According to the US Press Freedom Tracker, in 2020–2021 433 journalists were assaulted and 155 arrested in the United States. No civil liberty remains won.

7   Religion

Why does the First Amendment treat religion as the first among civil liberties, even before freedom of speech?

American history provides insight. During the colonial era, the Church of England was the establishment church in the southern colonies, with clergy appointed by and accountable to colonial authorities. Colonists were required to pay taxes to support that Church and were sometimes required to attend church. Other religions were not welcome. Thomas Jefferson objected to the fact that in Virginia, for example, religious minorities were not allowed to hold office and could be deprived of their property.

Settlers in the colonies, many of whom had emigrated to escape religious persecution, observed a variety of religions. In various colonies there were communities of Puritans, Quakers, Lutherans, Roman Catholics, and some settlements of Jews. While some enjoyed the opportunity to have their own religion dominate in a particular area, others chafed at official lack of tolerance for their religions and the fact that their tax dollars were used to support a religion other than their own. In deciding what values the Constitution should embrace some, like Patrick Henry, advocated continuing the special status of the Anglican Church. But most agreed that the United States of America should have no established church and should allow people to be free from federal interference with their choice of religion, resulting in the two religion clauses of the Bill of Rights: the Establishment Clause and the Free Exercise Clause ('Congress shall make no law respecting an establishment of religion, or prohibiting the free exercise thereof'). Both of those provisions were later incorporated and applied to the states as well.[1]

---

[1]   Cantwell v. Connecticut, 310 U.S. 296 (1940) (incorporating free exercise of religion); Everson v. Board of Education, 330 U.S. 1 (1947) (incorporating the Establishment Clause, a decision still not unanimously accepted).

The United States has historically been a highly religious country.[2] The liberty of individual conscience has often been viewed through the filter of religious belief. James Madison, in supporting Jefferson's objection to the lack of religious freedom in Virginia, said, 'It is the duty of every man to render to the Creator such homage, and such only, as he believes to be acceptable to him. This duty is precedent both in order of time and degree of obligation, to the claims of Civil Society.'[3]

In Madison's description, freedom of conscience takes precedence over politics. And it logically comes before speech in the Constitution as it does in human experience. Constitutional scholar Burt Neuborne explains the First Amendment as a holistic 'chronologically organized blueprint of democracy in action.'[4] Ideas are first formed in an individual's conscience (connected in Madison's conception with religious thought), then articulated and shared through free speech, disseminated by a free press, amplified and turned into a political movement by free assemblies of people, and potentially absorbed into law through the petition clause. For the government to control any aspect of that process is to undermine the idea that we, the people, are supposed to be in control of the government.

Whether or not they are viewed as a sequence, the rights of the First Amendment are certainly interconnected. The freedom of religion protected in the First Amendment overlaps with free speech, as in the *Barnette* case (see Section 5.1), where the family's objection to saluting the flag was based on their beliefs as Jehovah's Witnesses. In the cases following *Scopes* (see Section 5.4), academic freedom to teach scientific theories some Christians found incompatible with their faith was supported by the

---

[2]   In a 2021 Pew poll of Americans, 63% of respondents identified themselves as Christian and 6% as non-Christian believers (1% Jewish, 1% Muslim, 1% Buddhist, 1%, Hindu, and 2% who identify with a wide variety of other faiths). The percentage of those who do not identify with a particular religion (20%) or who identify as atheists/agnostics (9%), as well as the percentage of those who describe themselves as not attending worship services regularly, has been increasing in recent years. Similarly, the percentage of Americans who describe religion as 'very important' in their lives has been shrinking (from 56% to 41% over the 14 years), as has the percentage of Christians (75% in 2011; 63% in 2021).

[3]   James Madison, Memorial and Remonstrance against Religious Assessments (1785), https://founders.archives.gov/documents/Madison/01-08-02-0163.

[4]   Burt Neuborne, *Madison's Music: On Reading the First Amendment* (New York: New Press, 2015).

prohibition on establishing religion. And as will become clear, the two religion clauses of the First Amendment, the Free Exercise Clause and the Establishment Clause, are inextricably conjoined.

7.1   Free exercise of religion

Like the principle of content neutrality in regulation of speech, assembly, and the press, the guarantee of the free exercise of religion is understood to mean at least that the government may not discriminate among people on the basis of their religious beliefs. Because choice of religion is an individual civil liberty, a state may not punish or exclude individuals because they have chosen the wrong religion. A state could not, for example, prohibit Muslims from running for office or applying for a particular job. It is so well accepted that explicit religious discrimination would be prohibited by the courts that it is difficult even to come up with actual contemporary examples of facially discriminatory laws.[5] Of course, the fact that religious discrimination is against the law does not mean that it does not exist as a matter of practice.

It is pointless to try to tease out what the constitutional guarantee of free exercise of religion, standing alone, would mean, because it does not stand alone. The Establishment Clause is in some respects an alternative explanation for many protections of religious freedom: individuals have the right to make their own decisions about religion; the government is prohibited from establishing or preferring any religion. The Fourteenth Amendment's overlapping guarantee of the equal protection of the laws contributes to the strength of the bedrock anti-discrimination principle.

First Amendment doctrine has been less clear and less consistent about the permissibility of laws that burden exercise of one's religious beliefs without intentionally discriminating. Should it count as religious discrimination if a state job would require work on a Friday or Saturday, thus making that job unavailable to people who observe their religion's Sabbath on that day? Should it count as government infringement of the free exercise of religion if a military dress code prohibits wearing

---

[5]   The Trump executive order known as the Muslim ban was directed at non-Americans, who do not share First Amendment rights: Section 7.2.

non-regulation head coverings and thereby prevents Jews from wearing yarmulkes or Sikhs from wearing turbans?

Just as the history of protection of freedom of speech and assembly featured unpopular speakers and ideas, battles over the degree of accommodation to afford religion have centered on people whose minority religious beliefs are not always well understood or respected. Legislators may consciously or unconsciously shape a law to accommodate the tenets of familiar religions. It is less likely that a law will burden Christians when most lawmakers are themselves Christian and may instinctively assume that people should not be required to work on Sundays or on Christmas Day. When Congress passed the Patient Protection and Affordable Care Act in 2010, it provided religious groups with an exemption to the general requirement that employers subscribe to employee health plans including coverage of some methods of contraception because it was well aware of the beliefs of the Catholic Church and other religious groups. Thus, the most notable Supreme Court cases about free exercise of religion have involved claims for accommodation made by Jehovah's Witnesses, Seventh Day Adventists, Mormons, and Native Americans – religions practiced by small fractions of Americans.

As early as 1878, the Supreme Court posited that religious affiliation would not provide a basis for exemption from criminal laws. George Reynolds was a member of the Church of Jesus Christ of the Latter-Day Saints, also known as the Mormon Church. Reynolds was convicted of the offense of bigamy and argued that this prosecution violated his right to follow the tenets of his religion, which promoted plural marriage. The Court announced that the freedom of religion is not absolute, and that its scope is not to be determined by the individual believer. 'Laws are made for the government of actions, and while they cannot interfere with mere religious belief and opinions, they may with practices.'[6] To rule otherwise, the Court reasoned, would make 'the professed doctrines of religious belief superior to the law of the land, and in effect to permit every citizen to become a law unto himself.'

During the 1960s and 1970s, the Court modified this position and ramped up protection for religiously inspired conduct, requiring in some cases that a state demonstrate a compelling interest in order to hold people to

---

[6]   Reynolds v. United States, 98 U.S. 145 (1879).

general rules that have the impact of interfering with their religion. The Court found, for example, that Amish families could not be punished for disobeying a law requiring that they send their teenage children to school,[7] and that a Seventh Day Adventist could not be denied unemployment benefits for refusing a job that would have required her to work on her Sabbath (Saturday).[8]

In 1990, the Court reverted to the idea that the Free Exercise Clause 'does not relieve an individual of the obligation to comply with a valid and neutral law of general applicability on the ground that the law proscribes (or prescribes) conduct that his religion prescribes (or proscribes).'[9] The *Smith* case involved two Native American men who were fired from their jobs for using the drug peyote as part of a religious ritual and then denied unemployment compensation on the ground that the use of peyote in violation of state drug laws constituted disqualifying 'misconduct.' The Court held that plaintiffs like Smith would have a claim that their religious rights had been violated only if the law in question was intentionally passed in order to limit their freedom of religion. Thus, for example, a general law prohibiting cruelty to animals could constitutionally be applied to people whose religion (like the religion Santeria) requires ritual animal sacrifice. But if the motivation behind that law was not to protect animal welfare but rather to intimidate a disfavored religion, then the law will be considered to violate the Free Exercise Clause.[10]

The idea that religious practices must bow to laws of general applicability has been criticized by some as unduly limiting religious freedom, and also as unevenly affecting people whose religious beliefs are not mainstream. New Mexico law could have included an exemption for use of peyote as part of a religious ritual, but did not; the City of Hialeah, Florida could have enacted an animal cruelty statute that would have exempted religious rituals of animal sacrifice. But the New Mexico legislators may have been oblivious or hostile to the Native American religion affected.

---

[7]   Wisconsin v. Yoder, 406 U.S. 205 (1972).
[8]   Sherbert v. Verner, 374 U.S. 398 (1963).
[9]   Employment Division v. Smith, 494 U.S. 872 (1990).
[10]   Church of the Lukumi Babalu Aye v. City of Hialeah, 508 U.S. 520 (1993). The Hialeah ordinances at issue were enacted after it was announced that a Santeria house of worship was going to be built in that city. Chapter 11 discusses a similar distinction in equal protection law, drawing a consequential distinction between a law's intent and its discriminatory impact.

Hialeah aggressively used an ostensible concern about animals in an attempt to try to drive out a disfavored house of worship.

As the Court said in the *Reynolds* case, it is problematic to give individuals a veto over laws considered to be in the public interest. *Smith* committed the courts to defer to the goals of legislatures by not entertaining religious objections that might interfere with a law's enforcement, whether the law in question is a family law, health law, or civil rights law. But the pendulum swung again and Congress and the Court have become more accommodationist in recent years.

In the Religious Freedom Restoration Act of 1993 (RFRA), Congress attempted to restore the special protections for religion sometimes recognized in pre-*Smith* cases. RFRA (Section 3) prohibited:

> any agency, department, or official of the United States or any State (the government) from substantially burdening a person's exercise of religion even if the burden results from a rule of general applicability, except that the government may burden a person's exercise of religion only if it demonstrates that application of the burden to the person: (1) furthers a compelling governmental interest; and (2) is the least restrictive means of furthering that compelling governmental interest.

The Supreme Court found this statute unconstitutional because it asserted too much federal authority over the states.[11] Pushing back, Congress adopted a scaled back version of RFRA that applies only to *federal* agencies, departments, and officials, and also enacted a new statute, the Religious Land Use and Institutionalized Persons Act, that provides religious institutions (like the church at issue in the Supreme Court case) and prisoners a tool to fight back against state actions that would unnecessarily limit their religious freedom.

The revised version of RFRA became the basis for a challenge to a provision of the Affordable Care Act (ACA). The statute provided an exemption to contraceptive coverage for religious employers and institutions, like churches or other not-for-profit religious organizations, but the exemption did not cover for-profit employers whose religious beliefs opposed contraception devices. Hobby Lobby, a national arts and crafts chain with 500 stores around the country and over 13,000 employees, was

---

[11]   City of Boerne v. Flores, Archbishop of San Antonio, 521 U.S. 507 (1997).

owned by a deeply religious Christian family who described their business as being organized around biblical precepts, including belief in the immorality of forms of contraception they regarded as the equivalent of abortion. Under the *Smith* principle, Hobby Lobby had no First Amendment basis for challenging the obligation the law imposed on them. There is no First Amendment right to refuse to follow the requirements of a law of general applicability. But Hobby Lobby brought a lawsuit and won under the more solicitous provisions of RFRA.[12] The Justices split 5–4 on the issue of whether Hobby Lobby was actually covered by the provisions of RFRA, and on the potential breadth of the invitation not only to religious believers but also to corporations closely held by religious believers to claim exemptions from other laws of general applicability – including anti-discrimination laws.

In cases after *Hobby Lobby*, the increasingly conservative Supreme Court became increasingly reluctant to require people with religious claims of conscience to follow laws of general applicability, leaving the future of the *Smith* decision uncertain. The highly notorious *Masterpiece Cakeshop* case[13] involved a claim by a baker that he had a right, based on his religious beliefs, to refuse to bake a wedding cake that would be used in a celebration of the marriage of two men. The baker, Jack Phillips, said that he believed that decorating cakes is a form of art through which he can honor God and that it would displease God for him to create cakes for same-sex marriages. He less elegantly declared that he would rather bake a cake for two dogs. The Colorado Civil Rights Commission found that the bakery had discriminated against the customers, Charlie Craig and David Mullins, in violation of a Colorado civil rights law that prohibited discrimination on the basis of sexual orientation.

The case seemed to set up a stark contest between the state anti-discrimination law and the religious beliefs of the baker. The federal statute favoring religious rights, RFRA, did not apply because a state rather than a federal agency was involved, so the approach of the *Hobby Lobby* case was not available. The case seemed to force the Court to decide whether to overrule or modify *Smith*. But the Court found a way to avoid choosing between the liberty rights of the baker and the equality rights of the

---

12   Burwell v. Hobby Lobby Stores, Inc., 573 U.S. 682 (2014).
13   Masterpiece Cakeshop v. Colorado Civil Rights Commission, 584 U.S. ___ (2018).

wedding couple. Scrutinizing the background facts, the majority found that members of the Colorado Civil Rights Commission, in reaching their decision that Phillips had violated the state law, had made statements expressing hostility to his religious beliefs. Thus, the Court reasoned, Phillips had not been treated neutrally at the hearing on whether he had violated the state law, which was a contestable issue at the time. Colorado had treated him in a discriminatory manner because of the nature of his religious beliefs.

In the 2021 case of *Fulton v. City of Philadelphia*,[14] the Court continued to show its willingness to limit the *Smith* principle if there was any way to describe the facts of a case as showing a failure of neutrality on the part of the state. As in *Masterpiece Cakeshop*, on one side of the case was a general anti-discrimination policy that clearly had not been motivated by a desire to target religion or a particular religion: the City of Philadelphia's policy of not discriminating against same-sex couples who were being considered as foster parents. On the other side was an agency, Catholic Social Services, asserting that it would violate their religious beliefs to place children with a same-sex couple. Citing the agency's refusal to follow the anti-discrimination policy, Philadelphia refused to contract with Catholic Social Services to place children in foster homes.

As in *Masterpiece Cakeshop*, the Court focused on the facts of the case to avoid a showdown with *Smith*. Philadelphia's policy was said not to be neutral and generally applicable within the meaning of *Smith* because it allowed for exceptions to the anti-discrimination requirement at the sole discretion of the Commissioner. Having conveniently decided that *Smith* did not apply, the Court subjected the non-discrimination requirement to strict scrutiny. The city argued that its interest in its non-discrimination policy was compelling. But, the Court said, the question to be asked was not whether the city has a compelling interest in enforcing its non-discrimination policies generally, but whether it had such an interest in denying an exception to this particular agency. The majority concluded that it did not.

Although the narrow decision in the Philadelphia case was unanimous, three concurring Justices opined that the Court should have overruled

---

[14]   Fulton v. City of Philadelphia, 593 U.S. ___ (2021).

Smith, and other Justices seemed at least willing to consider whether that course would be advisable.

Pressure to overrule *Smith* is reduced by the Court's willingness to find that treatment of religious observers is not neutral in a wide variety of cases. In the case of a coach who wanted to say a public prayer at a football game despite school policy, a majority found that the school policy was not neutrally applied, as non-religious expressions would have been permitted while prayer was not, and so applied strict scrutiny to rule in favor of the coach.[15] In an earlier example, when the State of New York in 2020 sharply limited gatherings in order to prevent the spread of COVID-19, the Roman Catholic Diocese of Brooklyn and two Orthodox Jewish synagogues sought an injunction against application of the state's density restrictions to worship services.[16] The Supreme Court granted the injunction, with five Justices in the majority maintaining that religious institutions were being treated less favorably than stores selling what the state deemed "essentials," including wine and bicycles. Dissenting Justices argued that religious institutions were in fact being treated *more* favorably than comparable gatherings, given that concert and theater events were not being allowed at all.

Casting the facts, as in *Masterpiece Cakeshop*, as showing hostility to religion requires the state to pass the more demanding strict scrutiny test to apply neutral laws to religious organizations, giving those groups the power to undermine the state's goals.[17] An individual will have a greater ability to 'become a law unto himself.' Whether this is deemed a positive or negative development may simply depend on one's view of the primacy of religious observance.

7.2   Establishment of religion

That the First Amendment begins with the Establishment Clause ('Congress shall make no law respecting an establishment of religion')

---

[15]   Kennedy v. Bremerton School District, 597 U.S. ___ (2022). See Section 7.2.
[16]   Roman Catholic Diocese of Brooklyn v. Cuomo, 592 U. S. ___ (2020).
[17]   While the courts have not found any right for religious objectors to refuse vaccinations, state laws can provide for religious exemptions.

shows that the framers viewed this principle as paramount. But how this clause complements the Free Exercise Clause is far from clear.

The framers had different ideas about what goal this clause should serve, leading them to struggle over its language and to leave few clear guideposts for later interpretation. Some, like Thomas Jefferson, a deist, believed that there should be a wall between the Church and a secular state; some believed that the Church needed to be protected from interference by the state; others believed that state support of religion in general would not be problematic as long as the state did not prefer any particular religion.

These disparate points of view have been reflected by Supreme Court Justices endeavoring to create coherent law about what the Establishment Clause means beyond the principles already covered by the individual freedom of religion. In a 1947 case Justice Hugo Black provided a summary of what he thought the Establishment Clause means:

> Neither a state nor the Federal Government can set up a church. Neither can pass laws which aid one religion, aid all religions, or prefer one religion over another. Neither can force nor influence a person to go to or remain away from church against his will or force him to profess a belief or disbelief in any religion. No person can be punished for entertaining or professing religious beliefs or disbelief, for church attendance or non-attendance. No tax in any amount, large or small, can be levied to support religious activities or institutions, whatever they may be called, or whatever form they may adopt to teach or practice religion. Neither a state nor the Federal Government can, openly or secretly, participate in the affairs of any religious organizations or groups or vice versa. In the words of Jefferson, the clause against establishment of religion by law was intended to erect 'a wall of separation between church and State.'[18]

But in deciding the issue in the case – whether the state could provide buses to parochial schools – Black, although a free speech absolutist, thought there was room for accommodation for this use of tax dollars: buses, thought to be a safety measure, were provided to all regardless of their religious beliefs. Four Justices dissented, believing that allowing any public aid to parochial schools would become a slippery slope.

Another great Supreme Court civil libertarian, Justice William O. Douglas, also thought the Establishment Clause allowed some accommodation of

---

[18]   Everson v. Board of Education, 330 U.S. 1 (1947).

religion, including allowing public school children to be released from study hall in order to attend outside religious lessons. When the government 'encourages religious instruction or cooperates with religious authorities by adjusting the schedule of public events to sectarian needs, it follows the best of our traditions' by respecting the 'religious nature of our people.' To do otherwise, he said, would 'show a callous indifference to religious groups.'[19]

The Court continued to struggle with the question of whether the Establishment Clause should be understood to establish a wall between church and state, and whether it requires the state to be wholly neutral toward religion or only neutral with respect to an individual's choice of religion. Some issues proved easier to settle than others. The Court's conclusion that the Establishment Clause barred the state from prohibiting the teaching of evolution, or requiring the teaching of religious doctrine as a companion to teaching science, has already been described in Section 5.4. On the other hand, the courts have not objected to pervasive symbols of the country's deism, like the inclusion of the words 'one Nation under God' in the Pledge of Allegiance and the announcement at the beginning of each Supreme Court session: 'God save the United States and this Honorable Court!'

The question of what forms of assistance a state may constitutionally provide to religious schools has been far more contentious. Is it treating religion equally to provide religious schools with benefits provided to public schools (like free textbooks), or is it an improper breach of the principle that public money may not be used to support religion? Is providing equal support a benefit to religion, or would failure to provide equal support constitute a burden on religion? The most difficult situations here, too, are those in which the free exercise guarantee and the Establishment Clause seem to pull in opposite directions. For example, may or must a city allow groups to install a religious symbol, like a creche or menorah, in a public holiday display where non-religious symbols are allowed?

In 1971, the Supreme Court developed a multi-factor test to apply in such cases. The so-called *Lemon* test asked: 1) if a statute has a secular purpose; 2) if the principal or primary effect is one that neither advances

---

[19]   Zorach v. Clauson, 343 U.S. 306 (1952).

nor inhibits religion; and 3) whether the statute fosters 'an excessive government entanglement with religion.'[20] That test did not succeed in bridging the divide between separationists and accommodationists. By 2022, a majority of the Court abandoned the *Lemon* test and announced that instead the courts should look to history and tradition for guidance in deciding individual cases.[21]

That decision came in a case concerning the emotionally charged issue of school prayer. The Supreme Court had decided in the 1960s that involvement of public schools in religious activity, whether prayer or Bible readings, was contrary to the Establishment Clause – even if the prayer was non-denominational, and if students could be excused.[22] People who disagreed with this conclusion felt so strongly about school prayer that amendments to the Constitution to overturn the Court's rulings were proposed on numerous occasions, although they never garnered enough support to come close to adoption. The debate over school prayer was frequently muddled because students do have a free exercise right to pray in school or talk about their religion at school occasions like football games or graduations, but because of the Establishment Clause, the school itself may neither promote nor degrade religious exercise.

The Court blurred that line in 2022, opening the door to school prayer and generally weakening the Establishment Clause.[23] A majority sided with the high school football coach who claimed the right to pray midfield following football games, finding that the school's desire to avoid the appearance that the prayer was school-sponsored was trumped by the coach's free exercise and free speech rights. The school's evidently earnest attempt at Establishment Clause neutrality by not having a sports event be dominated by a Christian prayer was characterized as hostility to religion. The wall between church and state, meant to protect everyone's religious choices, was giving way to individual claims of freedom of religion. And, as in the recent free exercise cases, the result was set by a loaded description of the facts.[24]

---

20   Lemon v. Kurtzman, 403 U.S. 602 (1971).
21   Kennedy v. Bremerton School District, 597 U.S. ___ (2022).
22   Engel v. Vitale, 370 U.S. 421 (1962); School District of Abington Township v. Schempp, 374 U.S. 203 (1963).
23   Kennedy v. Bremerton School District, 597 U.S. ___ (2022).
24   The dissenters vigorously disagreed with the majority's characterization of the coach as praying quietly while the students were otherwise occupied,

On the whole, with free expression claims being taken more seriously and Establishment Clause claims minimized, the balance of the two religion clauses has shifted, with individual religious rights in the ascendancy.

One way in which the Establishment Clause is distinct from the Free Exercise Clause is that it declares a limitation on government rather than an individual right.[25] This means that government is prevented from favoring a particular religion or religion itself even if the individual people affected do not have a constitutional right at stake. For example, the travel ban President Donald Trump issued shortly after taking office in 2020 originally singled out people from Muslim countries for special restrictions on emigrating to the United States, and excused Christians in predominantly Muslim countries from those same restrictions. Trump's public comments explaining the ban were distinctly anti-Muslim. Even though the non-Americans affected by that order are not considered to have rights under the US Constitution, government is nevertheless prohibited by the Establishment Clause from adopting policies that favor one religion over another.

The Supreme Court upheld a somewhat revised version of the travel ban, dividing on the question of whether the ban actually did violate the Establishment Clause.[26] The dissenters thought the animus shown to Muslims constituted an Establishment Clause violation, disfavoring adherents to a particular religion on the basis of their religious beliefs. But because the president claimed that the ban would promote national security, a majority of the Court deferred to his decision despite the biased comments.

---

pointing out that the prayer took place at the fifty-yard line immediately following the game, the coach was joined by players and members of the public, and the coach had a history of ministering religion to the players. All the Justices agreed that the coach, like any school employee, would have had a right to pray if his prayer had indeed been personal and private.

[25]   Despite the language of the Establishment Clause, which is directed to Congress, the Clause has been found to apply to actions by the Executive branch as well, and to be incorporated against the states.

[26]   Trump v. Hawaii 585 U.S. ___ (2018).

8 Security against unreasonable searches and seizures

'Uncontrolled search and seizure is one of the first and most effective weapons in the arsenal of every arbitrary government,' according to Supreme Court Justice Robert H. Jackson, who also served as a prosecutor in the Nuremberg war crimes tribunal. 'Among deprivations of rights, none is so effective in cowing a population, crushing the spirit of the individual and putting terror in every heart ... the human personality deteriorates and dignity and self-reliance disappear where homes, persons and possessions are subject at any hour to unheralded search and seizure by the police.'[1]

The Fourth Amendment prohibits unreasonable searches and seizures in order to prevent the evils of an oppressive police state. The terms 'searches' and 'seizures' cover many different kinds of conduct by a wide variety of federal, state, and local law enforcement agents.[2] A search could be of a home, a car, a handbag, a cell phone, or a person being arrested. An intrusive search could entail tearing apart someone's home or car; a more superficial frisk is limited to seeing if a person temporarily detained is carrying a weapon. A person might be seized by an arrest or by a brief stop while the police issue a traffic ticket or investigate a crime.

As with protection of free speech, the law must strike a balance, preventing unreasonable exercises of power without unduly preventing the police from controlling crime. Professor Herbert Packer posited that people will be inclined to strike that balance differently depending on whether they

---

[1]   Brinegar v. United States, 338 U.S. 160 (1949).
[2]   I will use the word 'police' as a general term referring to a wide range of law enforcement agents.

are more concerned about crime control or about due process.[3] As will be discussed in Section 8.5, this dichotomy omits the important dimension of equality: minorities, especially Black men, pay a greater price when police are allowed broad discretion. Too many Americans are willing to accept the premises of the crime control model – that it is undesirable to 'handcuff' the police – because they expect the police to keep them and their property safe from crime and doubt that they themselves will be subject to unjustifiable searches or seizures.

Because appearing to be tough on crime tends to be a politically popular stance with a majority of voters, elected officials have generally been unwilling to limit police discretion. Thus it has for the most part fallen to the courts to police the police, especially to the politically insulated federal courts through interpretation of the Fourth Amendment. Like the First Amendment's protection of minority points of view, the Fourth Amendment guarantee of rights is counter-majoritarian. That is, the courts are expected to uphold the values it serves regardless of what a majority of people and their elected officials favor. And as in the First Amendment area, the courts have established constitutional rules by developing a cobweb of definitions, categorization, balancing tests, and exceptions.

During the 1960s, the Warren Court used these tools to expand Fourth Amendment protections substantially, as will be described. But beginning in the 1970s and accelerating through the twenty-first century, changes in composition of the Supreme Court resulted in lowering the floor of federal constitutional protection.

Law enforcement in the United States is highly balkanized. Federal, state, and local law enforcement agencies are all governed by their own jurisdictions' laws, regulations, and judicial rulings, which can provide protections beyond what the Fourth Amendment requires. The level of protection against arbitrary searches and seizures now varies considerably from state to state. But as will be explained, Fourth Amendment case law utterly fails to prevent or even address the problem of discriminatory enforcement and most states have not done much better on that front.

---

[3]   Herbert Packer, The Limits of the Criminal Sanction (Redwood City, CA: Stanford University Press, 1968).

8.1   Anglo-American history

In drafting the Bill of Rights provision addressing searches and seizures, the framers drew on both negative and positive experiences under English rule. On the negative side, the colonists had chafed at intrusive searches for radical papers and searches to enforce customs and other duties they regarded as a form of taxation without representation. The officials conducting searches were authorized to do so by various types of warrants, but the purpose of those warrants was not to protect anyone's liberty or privacy, but rather to protect the king's officers from civil lawsuits for trespass.

Colonists complained bitterly about the use of general warrants, which authorized royal officers to conduct open-ended searches to enforce seditious libel laws. The warrants were general in that they did not specify what goods or persons were to be the subject of a search, allowing those executing the warrant to search any part of a person's premises and to scrutinize and seize whatever they wished, including private papers and documents. Also detested were the writs of assistance used to enforce customs laws. These writs, similar to general warrants in the breadth of searches they allowed, delegated permanent and absolute discretion to decide where and what to search, and commanded all officers and subjects of the Crown to assist in those searches.

The colonists' complaints about unrestrained search and seizure as a form of tyranny were a major factor contributing to the American Revolution. When King George II died in 1760, his regime's authorization for writs of assistance expired six months after his death. Sixty-three Boston merchants hired a lawyer, James Otis, to argue against renewal of the writs of assistance. Otis gave an impassioned speech arguing that Magna Carta and the traditional rights of Englishmen were inconsistent with this level of government prerogative. John Adams, who was in the audience, said of that occasion, 'Then and there was the first scene of the first Act of opposition to the Arbitrary claims of Great Britain. Then and there the Child Independence was born.'[4]

---

[4]   Nelson B. Lasson, *The History and Development of the Fourth Amendment to the United States Constitution* (Baltimore, MD: Johns Hopkins Press, 1937); Jacob W. Landynski, *Search and Seizure and the Supreme Court:*

On the positive side, eighteenth-century English law had been developing protections against arbitrary searches. Parliament was turning against the use of general warrants. The English courts were imposing a series of requirements for the use of common law warrants authorizing searches for stolen goods: a judicial officer had to authorize the warrant, the warrant had to be based upon probable cause (a quantum of individualized suspicion), and the warrant had to specify the object of the search.

The most famous eighteenth-century English case, *Entick v. Carrington*,[5] established many of the principles we now take to be fundamental to civil liberties, especially the idea that executive authority must be exercised consistently with law. The Earl of Halifax had issued a warrant to search writer John Entick's home for seditious papers because Entick was connected with a controversial weekly newsletter that published allegedly libelous material. Carrington and three others executed the warrant by forcibly breaking into Entick's house and then spending four hours ransacking the house, breaking locks, causing considerable property damage, reading his papers, and seizing hundreds of papers and charts. Entick estimated the damage they caused as amounting to 2,000 pounds, the equivalent of close to 400,000 dollars today.

When Entick brought a lawsuit for trespass, the defending officers argued that such executive warrants had traditionally been considered valid to authorize searches of homes. The 1765 court held that the officers were not allowed to enter Entick's house because, although they did have a warrant, the warrant was not legally authorized. Lord Camden's landmark opinion announced, 'it is high time to put an end to [the use of unauthorized warrants], for if they are held to be legal, the liberty of this country is at an end.' Such power cannot be exercised, said the court, 'unless such exercise of it is authorised by some specific rule of law.' *Entick* was a new incarnation of Magna Carta's principle of legality: that government officials, including the king, are not above the law. The opinion also endorsed the idea that under traditional English law, the property of every man is 'held sacred.' As seventeenth-century English jurist Sir Edward Coke had declared, 'a man's home is his castle.' The

---

   A Study in Constitutional Interpretation (Baltimore, MD: Johns Hopkins Press, 1966).
5   Entick v. Carrington, 19 Howell's State Trials 1029 (1765).

Entick court valued individual liberty more highly than the prerogative of the Crown to stifle what it viewed as dangerous libel.

The framers of the Fourth Amendment were impressed, and designed the Fourth Amendment to affirm the result in *Entick* and reverse the result in the Writs of Assistance case.

8.2   The warrant requirement

The constitutional amendment the framers distilled from this history says:

> The right of the people to be secure in their persons, houses, papers, and effects, against unreasonable searches and seizures, shall not be violated [*the reasonableness clause*], and no Warrants shall issue, but upon probable cause, supported by Oath or affirmation, and particularly describing the place to be searched, and the persons or things to be seized [*the warrant clause*].[6]

Addressing the problem of unconstrained discretion that troubled the colonists, the warrant clause imposes predicates for permission to search: warrants must be based on probable cause and they must circumscribe the scope of the search or seizure. Warrants are issued by neutral and detached magistrates who are expected to provide an objective second opinion on whether an officer has enough basis for thinking that evidence of criminality will be found in the place to be searched, and on how broad a search or seizure is appropriate under the circumstances. As Justice Robert Jackson explained, police involved in the 'often competitive enterprise of ferreting out crime'[7] may engage in wishful or hasty thinking and thus may not be sufficiently objective.

Although the relationship between the warrant clause and the reasonableness clause is not grammatically clear, the Supreme Court decided during the 1960s, the era of maximal Fourth Amendment protection, that the warrant clause was to be regarded as dominant, creating a presump-

---

[6]   For a detailed explication of Fourth Amendment law, see Wayne R. LaFave, *Search and Seizure: A Treatise on the Fourth Amendment* (Eagan, MN: Thomson Reuters West, 6th edition, 2020).

[7]   Johnson v. United States, 333 U.S. 10 (1948).

tion that a search is unreasonable unless a warrant has been obtained.[8] Prior approval is preferable to post hoc evaluation by a court for several reasons. First, if a search is unjustified, it is better to prevent the intrusion from taking place than to consider after the fact whether the intrusion was a mistake. Second, as a practical matter, whether police have a good enough reason to search can be evaluated objectively only before the search takes place. After a search that uncovers something criminal, it is very difficult to ignore the fact that pre-search suspicions, no matter how ill-founded, actually turned out to be true.

Not all Justices or scholars have accepted the interpretation of the Fourth Amendment as imposing a preference for warrants as opposed to a more open-ended reasonableness approach.[9] Enough other Justices have been ambivalent that the warrant requirement has almost been eclipsed by a proliferation of exceptions. The Court has found that warrants are almost never required before an arrest (a highly intrusive form of seizure).[10] And the Court has created categorical exceptions to the search warrant requirement for searches of vehicles, searches incident to arrest, and so on. These exceptions are generally based on the idea that there are exigent circumstances in certain situations that would make it impossible or inappropriate to require law enforcement officers to get a warrant before conducting a search. But the Court's theoretical bright line rules sometimes clash with reality. For example, the so-called automobile exception, which allows the search of a vehicle without a warrant, was announced in a 1925 case, partly based on the theory that because automobiles are mobile it would not be feasible for an officer to leave the scene and consult a magistrate to get permission to conduct a search.[11] Either the motorist would have to be detained for a lengthy period of time or the officer's opportunity to search would evaporate. A century later,

---

[8] Chimel v. California, 395 U.S. 752 (1969).

[9] Historian Telford Taylor argued that the Fourth Amendment was not intended to create a preference for warrants, in *Two Studies in Constitutional Interpretation* (Columbus, OH: Ohio State University Press, 1969). Justice Antonin Scalia remained committed to the idea that the reasonableness clause should be dominant.

[10] United States v. Watson, 423 U.S. 411 (1976).

[11] Carroll v. United States, 267 U.S. 132 (1925). The other rationale for the automobile exception is that one cannot reasonably expect privacy in an automobile because automobiles are heavily regulated and, unlike homes, travel through public places.

the advent of telephones and computers in police cars has made it quite feasible for an officer to consult a magistrate promptly without leaving the scene. Nevertheless, the blanket automobile exception, having outlived a major part of its rationale, survives.

The warrant requirement has been taken most seriously with respect to searches of people's homes – still regarded as private castles. The Court has required that warrants be obtained before bringing a drug-sniffing dog onto the porch of a person suspected of growing illegal marijuana,[12] before using a thermal imaging device to detect whether a suspect was growing marijuana inside his home,[13] and before arresting a person in their home.[14] In this context, originalists interpret the Fourth Amendment expansively on the basis of English common law giving property owners special rights.[15] But focusing on property rights can lead to inequities: do public housing residents have no right to be free from police dogs sniffing at their doors because they do not own the hallway? In the so-called 'war on drugs,' arrests for drug offenses have been racially skewed, perhaps partly because people who spend more time on the streets and in their cars are easy targets while people who sell and use illegal drugs behind doors and gates they own are not.

8.3   What is a 'search'?

A lot depends on what the Court defines as a 'search' or 'seizure.' Not every law enforcement capture of a person's private information is regarded as a 'search' triggering Fourth Amendment protections; not every confrontation with police is regarded as a 'seizure.' The Supreme Court's often bizarrely limiting interpretations of these terms have narrowed the number of circumstances where the procedural protections of the Fourth Amendment, including both the warrant requirement and the reasonableness requirement, will apply. Definitional issues have been par-

---

[12]   Florida v. Jardines, 569 U.S. 1 (2013).
[13]   Kyllo v. United States, 533 U.S. 27 (2001).
[14]   Payton v. New York, 445 U.S. 573 (1980).
[15]   For a critique of reliance on common law in interpreting the Fourth Amendment, see David Sklansky, The Fourth Amendment and Common Law (2000) 100 *Columbia Law Review* 1739.

ticularly problematic in the context of cases involving new technologies, from automobiles,[16] to cell phones, to datamining.

As mentioned in the Introduction, the Court confronted the question of whether telephone wiretapping is a search or seizure within the meaning of the Fourth Amendment in 1928. A majority of the Court in *Olmstead v. United States*[17] adopted a formalistic, originalist view of the Fourth Amendment's words, holding that the phrase 'persons, houses, papers, and effects' was intended to cover only physical invasions – the only type of search or seizure the framers would have envisioned. Therefore the Court concluded that the Constitution had nothing to say about the conduct of the federal agents involved, even though those agents had violated a state law with their investigative methods.

Justice Louis Brandeis's much-celebrated dissent adopted a more generous view of the meaning of the Fourth Amendment, based on a different philosophy of the nature of the Constitution. The Fourth Amendment, he said, should be read along with other aspects of the Bill of Rights as protecting a broad 'right to be let alone.' See Section 1.4.

Brandeis viewed this case as demonstrating the necessity of adapting the Fourth Amendment to technological developments. Critical civil liberties protections, he said, should not hinge on 'the form that evil had theretofore taken.' It is obvious even to originalists today that the First Amendment should be considered to protect speech on the Internet, which did not exist in the eighteenth century. It was equally obvious to Brandeis that the particular words of the Fourth Amendment should not be read so narrowly as to allow the government to take advantage of loopholes created by technological advances. He saw telephone wiretapping as merely a subtler and more far-reaching means of governmental invasion of privacy than physical searches. Invoking *Entick v. Carrington*'s condemnation of entering a home to seize private papers, Brandeis uncannily foresaw that '[w]ays may some day be developed by which the Government, without removing papers from secret drawers, can reproduce them in court.'

---

[16]   Sarah A. Seo, *Policing the Open Road: How Cars Transformed American Freedom* (Cambridge, MA: Harvard University Press, 2019).
[17]   Olmstead v. United States, 277 U.S. 438 (1928).

A decade after *Olmstead*, New York provided an example of how a state can build on the federal constitutional floor by amending its state constitution to require that state officials obtain a warrant before intercepting telephone or telegraph communications.[18]

Four decades after *Olmstead*, a limited version of Brandeis's view prevailed in *Katz v. United States*,[19] where the Court reversed *Olmstead*'s holding and decided that the government should be required to obtain a warrant before wiretapping a telephone. The Court declared that the Fourth Amendment protects 'people, not places,' and found that Charles Katz had a reasonable expectation of privacy in his telephone conversation despite the fact that he had been using a public telephone booth.

Since then the Court has used the concept of the reasonable expectation of privacy as its standard in deciding whether government conduct amounts to a search. But this test has sometimes been applied in surprising ways to keep the Fourth Amendment from limiting government investigations. The 'third-party doctrine,' for example, holds that it does not count as a search if government demands records or personal information from a third party with whom their target has shared that information. This concept was first applied to financial records, because customers have shared the underlying financial information with a bank,[20] and to telephone numbers (of calls placed or received) one has shared with the telephone company.[21] By sharing information, the Court opined, one assumes the risk that the bank or telephone company might reveal it to someone else and therefore one has no reasonable expectation of privacy.

---

[18]   New York State Constitution, Article I Section 12 (1938): 'The right of the people to be secure in their persons, houses, papers and effects, against unreasonable searches and seizures, shall not be violated, and no warrants shall issue, but upon probable cause, supported by oath or affirmation, and particularly describing the place to be searched, and the persons or things to be seized ... The right of the people to be secure against unreasonable interception of telephone and telegraph communications shall not be violated, and ex parte orders or warrants shall issue only upon oath or affirmation that there is reasonable ground to believe that evidence of crime may be thus obtained, and identifying the particular means of communication, and particularly describing the person or persons whose communications are to be intercepted and the purpose thereof.'

[19]   Katz v. United States, 389 U.S. 347 (1967).

[20]   Miller v. United States, 425 U.S. 435 (1976).

[21]   Smith v. Maryland, 442 U.S. 735 (1979).

The government's conduct in compelling a bank or telephone company to turn over private information, therefore, is not considered a 'search' and is not limited by anything in the Fourth Amendment.[22]

The third-party doctrine has increasingly been questioned by commentators and judges as we are all compelled, as a condition of participating in society, to share vast amounts of information about our private affairs or our whereabouts with not only banks, but schools, health care providers, Internet service providers, cell phone providers, etc. Some argue that legislatures are better positioned than courts to adopt appropriate constraints for emerging technologies. On some occasions, federal and state legislatures have been more willing than the courts to protect the privacy of records. Congress responded to the Supreme Court cases declining Fourth Amendment coverage to financial and telephone records by passing statutes protecting those records. Statutes also protect health, educational, and library records. But it is an understatement to say that Congress has not kept up to date with the threats to privacy posed by emerging technology. The Electronic Communications Privacy Act Congress enacted in 1986 has not been updated to take account of transformational technological developments since that date – like the Internet and the growth of location monitoring techniques.

The third-party doctrine and other loopholes the Court had created in Fourth Amendment coverage allowed Congress to give the government powerful 'tools required to intercept and obstruct terrorism' in the so-called war on terror. Much of the controversial USA Patriot Act,[23] which allowed the government to obtain records, tangible things, and information about particular people even without probable cause or any legitimate basis for suspicion, exploited the third-party doctrine by simply rescinding Congress's own statutory protections for various kinds

---

[22] Another consequence of the Court's focus on an individual's reasonable expectation of privacy is that government misconduct is not considered to violate the Fourth Amendment if it takes place outside the United States and involves non-US citizens who cannot claim constitutional rights. United States v. Verdugo-Urquidez, 494 U.S. 259 (1990).

[23] The statute's name is a backronym for 'Uniting and Strengthening America by Providing Appropriate Tools Required to Intercept and Obstruct Terrorism.'

of private records – including medical, educational, and library records – in terrorism investigations, leaving those records open to investigators.[24]

Anti-terrorism investigators took advantage of the absence of constitutional guardrails in many ways. Edward Snowden disclosed, for example, that the government had been secretly ordering telephone companies to turn over massive quantities of their customers' telephone metadata (telephone numbers one has called or received calls from) without any basis of suspicion, to trawl for evidence of terrorism. Access to this metadata, even though very revealing of private matters, was not considered to be a Fourth Amendment 'search.' After Snowden's revelations, a contemporary cartoon showed a bureaucrat saying to his staff, 'Get me everything on everybody.' But public reaction led to only minor changes in the law because a majority of Americans thought they would not really be giving up a significant amount of liberty or privacy in exchange for what the government portrayed as a possibility of greater safety. Why, many people asked, should I care what the government knows about me if I am not doing anything wrong?

Civil libertarians have answers to the question of why privacy matters. As Elaine Scarry eloquently said:

> The Patriot Act inverts the constitutional requirement that people's lives be private and the work of government officials be public; it instead crafts a set of conditions in which our inner lives become transparent and the workings of the government become opaque. Either one of these outcomes would imperil democracy; together they not only injure the country but also cut off the avenues of repair.[25]

8.4   What is a 'seizure'?

Defining what counts as a 'seizure' triggering Fourth Amendment protections raises comparable issues. The narrower the definition of seizure, the more unrestrained power law enforcement may exercise, creating a serious risk of arbitrary or discriminatory enforcement.

---

[24]   Susan N. Herman, The USA PATRIOT Act and the Submajoritarian Fourth Amendment (2006) 41 Harvard Civil Rights-Civil Liberties Law Review 67.

[25]   Elaine Scarry, Resolving to Resist (2004) (*Boston Review*, February 1, 2004).

In the 1968 case of *Terry v. Ohio*, the Court found that not only full-scale arrests but also temporary detentions can count as Fourth Amendment 'seizures.'[26] The liberal Warren Court declared that what came to be called '*Terry* stops' were reasonable even in the absence of either a warrant or probable cause, as long as they were brief and based on an articulable reasonable suspicion that criminal activity was afoot. In other words, officers were allowed to detain people as long as they could provide an explanation after the fact of what caused them to regard a particular person as suspicious. In the *Terry* case itself, an officer had suspected that Terry and his companions were casing a jewelry store with the intention of robbing it. The Court also ruled that during a *Terry* stop, an officer may frisk the person being detained if the officer has reason to believe the person may be armed and presently dangerous.

Warren sought to impose some limitations on the newly authorized power to stop and frisk, but at the same time conferred an enormous amount of discretion on law enforcement officers which has proved difficult to contain. There is no neutral and detached magistrate to provide a check before a stop or frisk. And courts reviewing stops after the fact have been quite permissive in defining what counts as 'reasonable suspicion.' In one case, for example, the Supreme Court held that Chicago police had sufficient reason to stop a man, Sam Wardlow, who ran away when a police caravan drove through what was said to be a high crime neighborhood.[27] The police knew no more than that – and it was not even clear that the caravan, which was unmarked, could be identified as a police vehicle. Sam Wardlow was Black.

If a stop and frisk does not result in finding a weapon or finding actual evidence of criminality, which is what happens in most instances, the suspects will be released and are unlikely to complain to a court about their treatment. Litigation is daunting and expensive. After Terry was found to have a gun, he was prosecuted and had a lawyer to challenge the constitutionality of his frisk. If Terry had not had a gun, it is unlikely

---

[26]   Terry v. Ohio, 392 U.S. 1 (1968). It is notable that the opinion in *Terry* was written by Chief Justice Earl Warren, famous for heading the most liberal Supreme Court in American history. Dissenting Justice Douglas expressed dismay at the permission *Terry* afforded for any seizure of a person not predicated on the existence of probable cause.

[27]   Illinois v. Wardlow, 528 U.S. 119 (2000).

that any court would have encountered his case – an innocent man who had been harassed by the police. Because the courts are less likely to see the many cases where an officer's allegedly reasonable suspicion turned out to be wrong, judges may have a mistaken subliminal impression that the police only stop people for good reason, bolstering their inclination to defer to the police.

In addition to making it fairly easy to justify stops, the courts have defined many police-initiated encounters as not being 'seizures' at all, and therefore not necessitating any justification or judicial review. To decide whether an individual has been 'seized,' the courts ask if a reasonable person in those circumstances would feel free to leave. The Supreme Court's applications of this general test, however, consider the perceptions of a hypothetical reasonable person who sometimes bears no resemblance to the parties involved in the case. In *United States v. Drayton*,[28] for example, the Court found that a passenger was not 'seized' when officers boarded his bus, told him that they were searching for drugs and weapons, questioned him, and asked to search his bag and his person without advising him that he had a right to decline consent.[29] The fact that Drayton agreed to the searches even though he had illicit drugs on his person suggests that he did not feel free to refuse. This bus 'sweep' was permitted even though the officers had no good reason to suspect Drayton of any misconduct. Christopher Drayton was Black.

Similarly, the Court found no seizure to have occurred in a case where workers in a Southern California garment factory were questioned by immigration officials who took over the workspace for one to two hours, stationing agents at the exits. The officials, wearing badges and carrying weapons, questioned all the employees about their immigration status.[30] The Court held that the circumstances of this interrogation would not be intimidating to a 'reasonable person,' even though it seems likely that reasonable employees of Mexican ancestry in that factory did indeed feel intimidated by these tactics. This factory survey was conveniently catego-

---

[28]   United States v. Drayton, 536 U.S. 194 (2002).
[29]   The Court has held that a consent to search may be regarded as voluntary even where officers have not advised the person of their right to refuse. Schneckloth v. Bustamonte, 412 U.S. 218 (1973).
[30]   INS v. Delgado, 466 U.S. 210 (1984).

rized as a consensual encounter rather than a seizure, and so the officials did not need to offer any justification for their overbearing conduct.

Applying a one-size-fits-all reasonable person standard ignores the different perspectives of racial minorities or recent immigrants confronted with aggressive police tactics. It also ignores the fact that police often choose to confront people like Sam Wardlow, Christopher Drayton, and the factory workers because of their race rather than their conduct, possibly as a result of unconscious bias. As in *Olmstead*, the Court stuck to the framers' conceptions of the rights they were protecting – like the exclusive rights of property owners – instead of reading the Fourth Amendment as flexible enough to address the contemporary problem of biased law enforcement in a multicultural country.

The courts in a few states have provided limitations on police discretion to intimidate people in circumstances where the Fourth Amendment is not available. The New York Court of Appeals, for example, devised a more nuanced common law approach to police-initiated encounters that is not wholly contingent on whether or not a police encounter is considered a 'seizure.' Under New York's four-tiered formulation, every encounter requires an appropriate level of justification.[31] Police are not allowed to stop a person without some legitimate reason, or to ask for consent to search – a bag, a person, a vehicle – unless they have some articulable reason for doing so. This formulation exposes dragnet tactics like bus sweeps or factory surveys to judicial review. But in most states, the courts and legislatures are no more zealous in addressing the problem of discriminatory enforcement than the Supreme Court.

---

[31] People v. DeBour, 40 N.Y.2d 210 (1976); People v. Hollman, 79 N.Y.2d 181 (1992). The test has four tiers: If a police officer seeks simply to request information from an individual, that request must be supported by an objective, credible reason, not necessarily indicative of criminality. The common law right of inquiry, a wholly separate level of contact, is 'activated by a founded suspicion that criminal activity is afoot and permits a somewhat greater intrusion.' Where a police officer has reasonable suspicion that a particular person was involved in a felony or misdemeanor, the officer is authorized to forcibly stop and detain that person. Finally, where the officer has probable cause to believe that a person has committed a crime, an arrest is authorized.

8.5   Liberty, crime control, and equality

It is axiomatic that delegation of discretion permits arbitrary or discriminatory law enforcement, whether the discrimination is conscious or unconscious.[32] And law enforcement in the United States is undeniably racially discriminatory at every stage of the process. People who are Black or Latino, especially Black men, are not only more likely to be stopped on the street but also to be stopped while driving, arrested, prosecuted, incarcerated, and executed.

As noted above, Herbert Packer's spectrum of crime control and due process omits a critical third perspective of equality. Willingness to trade one's own liberty for a chimera of safety might be short-sighted; willingness to give up someone else's liberty is a different matter entirely.

In reaching the conclusion in the bus sweep case that a reasonable person in those circumstances would have felt free to leave, the Court simply ignored the fact that Christopher Drayton was Black and may well have had a very different perception than a white passenger of his power to refuse a law enforcement agent's request. Four dissenters in the *Wardlow* case, in one of the first opinions recognizing that not everyone has the same reaction to the police, disagreed with the majority that it was reasonable to infer that because Sam Wardlow had run away from an encounter with the police, he was acting out of consciousness of guilt. As a Black man, Wardlow might well have had other reasons to run away – like wanting to avoid incipient criminal activity, wanting to avoid a showdown involving the police, or wanting to avoid the indignity of being regarded as a criminal suspect. But that was only a dissenting opinion.

The highest court in Massachusetts later picked up that theme and found that running from the police, without more, would not be regarded as suspicious conduct under Massachusetts law.[33] Citing a recent report finding that Black men in Boston had been disproportionately subjected to racial profiling, the court said, 'Such an individual, when approached by the police, might just as easily be motivated by the desire to avoid

---

[32]   Charles R. Lawrence III, The Id, the Ego, and Equal Protection: Reckoning with Unconscious Racism (1987) 39(2) *Stanford Law Review* 317.
[33]   Commonwealth v. Warren, 475 Mass. 530 (2016).

the recurring indignity of being racially profiled as by the desire to hide criminal activity.'

In New York City, a lawsuit challenging the New York Police Department's stop and frisk practices identified severe racial disparities: approximately 85 percent of those stopped were Black and Latino, even though these two groups make up only 52 percent of the city's population.[34] The challenged program was massive – 4.4 million stops were made between January 2004 and June 2012 – and had a low yield rate for discovering criminal offenses or weapons. In 88 percent of instances the stops did not result in further law enforcement action; 52 percent of the time people stopped were also frisked, but a weapon was found only 1.5 percent of the time. A federal district court concluded, after a nine-week trial, that the city had a '*policy* or *custom* of violating the Constitution by making unlawful stops and conducting unlawful frisks,'[35] which not only denied individual rights but also undermined community confidence in the police. A new mayor elected in 2013, Bill de Blasio, obviated an appeal by agreeing to implement reforms. In addition, the New York City Council enacted a Right to Know Act in 2018, requiring officers to identify themselves personally when they stop someone, to advise a person they ask for consent to a search that they have a right to decline, and to wear a body camera. Under the revised New York City policies, the volume of stops and frisks decreased, but issues about racialized law enforcement remained. Other cities also continue to struggle with similar problems.

Stop and frisk is far from the only instance of racialized law enforcement. And it is not the only area where the Court has abdicated from any role in trying to prevent discriminatory enforcement. The Court refused to impose any limits on police discretion to arrest people for traffic offenses,[36] for example, even if the traffic arrest was merely a pretext for exploring whether the people stopped might have illicit drugs.[37] The laws of some states, like Texas, allow police almost total discretion to decide when to arrest a driver for traffic violations rather than issue a citation.

---

34 Floyd v. City of New York, 959 F. Supp. 2d 540 (SDNY 2013) (emphasis in the original).

35 Ibid.

36 Atwater v. City of Lago Vista, 532 U.S. 318 (2001) allowed a custodial arrest, accompanied by a search incident to arrest, for violation of a seat belt law.

37 Whren v. United States, 517 U.S. 806 (1996).

Unless local law limits discretion to arrest, any motorist who drives a mile above the speed limit or fails to signal a turn may be taken into custody and searched, an enormous blank check for racial profiling.

The Court has also set a high bar for what constitutes police misconduct, ruling for example that an officer cannot be sued for recklessly causing a suspect's death in a high speed chase.[38] And when law enforcement officials do purposely and unconstitutionally employ unjustifiable or deadly force, they are frequently protected against lawsuits by the Court's expansive qualified immunity defense if they claim that they had not had sufficient advance warning that their particular actions were unconstitutional.

The murder of George Floyd by Minneapolis police officer Derek Chauvin in May of 2020 triggered a summer of mass protests – the largest in US history. A viral video taken by a bystander showed Chauvin blithely kneeling on Floyd's neck for nine minutes and 29 seconds while an increasingly desperate Floyd gasped for air. This shocking image caused many people to realize that the level of discretion exercised by police in the United States does indeed lead to racially disproportionate results, including the disproportionate use of deadly force. Many advocated defunding the police and allocating some of the role police had been playing to social service agencies. The angry reactions of some police to the demonstrations[39] added fuel to what seemed to be a growing consensus that police discretion needed to be controlled.

For the next several years, discussions around the country within police departments, in political venues, and among the public, mooted the possibility of reform and the proper role of the police. But time seemed to dull

---

[38] County of Sacramento v. Lewis, 523 U.S. 833 (1998).

[39] In many parts of the country, peaceful protesters were met with aggressive police responses including tear gassing and physical brutality. In Minneapolis itself, police fired tear gas and rubber bullets at crowds including peaceful protesters. Some of those actions were challenged as violations of the rights of the protesters, including the freedom of assembly. In one of the first cases to go to trial, a jury in Colorado awarded a $14 million verdict to Denver protesters who had been subject to indiscriminate use of excessive force. (See Colorado Jury Awards $14 Million to Demonstrators Injured in George Floyd Protests (New York Times, March 26, 2022) https://www .nytimes.com/2022/03/26/us/denver-george-floyd-protests-ruling.html. In Minneapolis itself, police fired tear gas and rubber bullets at crowds including peaceful protesters.

the sense of urgency and political reality set in. Reform through the political process was difficult to effect and unlikely to be effective. Minneapolis had previously been shown to engage in racist arrest practices and,[40] in response to public reaction, had adopted reform measures recommended by an Obama commission on policing. Those reforms did not sufficiently change police culture to prevent George Floyd's death.

The Court's permissive, colorblind Fourth Amendment law has failed to address the problems of unequal policing. Chapter 11 will discuss how and why the Court's colorblind equal protection caselaw has failed to pick up the slack.

[40]   See ACLU, Picking up the Pieces: Policing in America, a Minneapolis Case Study, https://www.aclu.org/issues/racial-justice/race-and-criminal-justice/picking-pieces?redirect=feature/picking-pieces (2015).

9   Due process of law

9.1   Rights of the accused in criminal proceedings

The most basic liberty is the right to be free of physical restraint. English law, based on the principles of Magna Carta, created a right of habeas corpus so that people could challenge the legality of their detention in court and also created procedural safeguards to prevent unjust imprisonment by the state. Those protections included the right to trial by jury, which William Blackstone referred to as the bulwark of civil liberty. The expectation was that a jury of one's peers would provide an effective check on abusive prosecutions.

The colonists took those rights very seriously, listing their complaints about being deprived of the right to trial by jury in the Declaration of Independence (see Section 2.2). No fewer than 22 provisions in the Constitution and Bill of Rights prescribe procedural rights and limitations the framers believed necessary to prevent the new federal government from abusing its power of arrest and prosecution.

In laying out the basic structure of the federal government, the original articles of the Constitution enumerated several kinds of procedural protections – like a right to trial by jury in Article III and a limitation on Congress's power to suspend the writ of habeas corpus in Article I. The Bill of Rights then added, in the Fifth Amendment, a Due Process Clause that bears some resemblance to Magna Carta's law of the land provision – no person shall 'be deprived of life, liberty, or property, without due process of law.' The Fifth Amendment added other specific procedural protections, including a privilege against self-incrimination (people could not be forced to testify against themselves) and a ban on being put twice in jeopardy for the same offense, and the Sixth Amendment added a series of rights guaranteed 'in all criminal prosecutions' to 'the accused.'[1] These rights were designed to counter potential shortcomings that could lead to an unfair conviction. An accused might be acquitted by a jury but then charged again for the same offense, perhaps repeatedly. Suspects might be compelled, by physical or legal means, to provide evidence against themselves, which might or might not be true. A trial might be delayed for so long that defense witnesses could have become unavailable or have their memories fade; a trial might be held in secret, shielding and thus inviting misdeeds by the prosecutor or judge; evidence might be misleadingly one-sided, because the accused was either unable to confront and cross-examine prosecution witnesses or unable to secure the testimony of people with testimony favorable to the defense.

There have, of course, been many issues about interpretation of these rights.[2] How should the courts assess when a public trial may be closed due to the presentation of sensitive information, perhaps relating to national security claims?[3] Must a jury verdict be unanimous? But as with the Fourth Amendment, the most vexing issues in this area have centered on the interplay of race and class in the criminal legal system. To what extent will the rights listed in the Bill of Rights provide sufficient protection for criminal defendants who, unlike the framers, are poor, non-English-speaking, or non-white?

As early as the 1930s, the Court decided that the Sixth Amendment right to counsel should be read to include a right for indigent criminal defendants in federal court to have free counsel assigned, in a case called *Johnson v. Zerbst*.[4] Because the government is represented by an attorney, and because the result of the trial may depend on complex legal issues difficult

---

[1] The Sixth Amendment guarantees the right of the accused to a speedy and public trial; the right to trial by an impartial jury of the state and district where the crime alleged was committed; the right to be informed of the nature and cause of the accusation; the right to be confronted with the witnesses against him and to have compulsory process for obtaining witnesses in his favor; and the right to have the assistance of counsel for his defense.

[2] See Christopher Slobogin, *Advanced Introduction to US Criminal Procedure* (Cheltenham, UK: Edward Elgar, 2020).

[3] Susan N. Herman, *The Right to a Speedy and Public Trial* (Westport, CT: Praeger, 3rd edition, 2006).

[4] Johnson v. Zerbst, 304 U.S. 458 (1938).

for a non-lawyer to understand, the Court thought convicting someone who was unrepresented was unfair.

This ruling, applicable at the time only to the federal government, came before the rise of modern originalism. Scholar James Tomkovicz suggests that originalists could have found a basis in history for resisting this progressive interpretation of the Sixth Amendment.[5] The evil that English law and the colonists were worried about preventing, in his account, was government interference with existing attorney-client relationships. The right to assigned counsel is one of very few instances where the Constitution has been found to impose any kind of affirmative obligation on government to reduce the impact of socioeconomic disparity. And the Court imposed this obligation without worrying about whether the authors of the Sixth Amendment had evinced any special concern for impoverished defendants.

Thus far, there has not been a major movement to reverse *Johnson v. Zerbst* or its 1963 extension to the states.[6] But the right to assigned counsel has not leveled the playing field in practice because states have not provided sufficient funding to pay for effective representation or allowed indigent clients a choice of counsel. Assigned counsel in public defenders' offices struggle under heavy caseloads, low pay, and inadequate resources to engage expert witnesses. The Court has interpreted the right to counsel as encompassing a right to the effective assistance of counsel, but the test under which the Court evaluates effectiveness[7] has been heavily criticized for being weighted toward excusing poor performance by counsel and ignoring the discrepancy between the typical class and race of counsel and of the defendants they represent.[8]

---

[5]   James J. Tomkovicz, *The Right to Assistance of Counsel* (Westport, CT: Praeger, 2002).

[6]   Gideon v. Wainwright, 372 U.S. 335 (1963).

[7]   Strickland v. Washington, 466 U.S. 668 (1984), lays out a two-pronged test: a defendant wishing to establish the ineffectiveness of counsel must show first, that the counsel's performance was objectively deficient (a standard difficult for defendants to meet in practice) and second, that there is a reasonable probability that representation by a competent attorney would have led to a different result.

[8]   Alexis J. Hoag, The Color of Justice (2022) April *University of Michigan Law Review*.

9.2 Federalism and due process in state criminal proceedings

As noted above, the eighteenth-century Bill of Rights only applied to the federal government, which the framers feared would be remote from the people's tempering influence, like the British Crown. But the federal government before the mid-twentieth century did not have extensive powers to criminalize and punish conduct. The vast majority of criminal prosecutions took place in state court. The states had their own constitutions, which generally provided a list of procedural rights in criminal prosecutions, often including 'law of the land' provisions, and often including rights overlapping with those secured against the federal government in the Bill of Rights. But the state protections were not consistent, either in theory or in practice. States could, if they wished, provide fewer rights than the Bill of Rights model, and many states could and did use criminal prosecution as a form of racial control.

After the Thirteenth Amendment abolished the institution of slavery in 1865, southern states where the institution of slavery had been in full force confronted the fact that they had large populations of Black people who were no longer subject to the harsh whips and chains of slavery. States sought to control the freed population through arrest, prosecution, and sometimes execution. They generated tools to expand police and prosecutorial discretion, including statutes authorizing arrest for the vague crime of 'vagrancy.' Vigilantes, sometimes joined by state employees, supplemented the criminal law by lynching thousands of Black men for imagined offenses, for peccadilloes like touching a white person, or for the offense of simply existing. State officials typically did nothing to prevent or punish private racist violence.

On those occasions when state officials cared to dissuade lynch mobs, they could reliably promise vigilantes that their target would be executed under the auspices of the law. Capital prosecutions of Black men were often tantamount to a lynching in a courtroom. The Fourteenth Amendment did require the states to afford due process of the law before depriving any person of life, liberty, or property – and state law often provided additional rights in theory – but the state courts too often failed to heed those guarantees when the accused was Black.

National intervention was needed to protect civil liberties, but no branch of the federal government actively addressed these horrific injustices for many decades. Although federal anti-lynching laws had been proposed many times over the years, Congress did not actually adopt such a law until 2022. The Department of Justice was slow to prosecute violators of existing Reconstruction era civil rights statutes. And the federal courts were reluctant to sit in judgment on the fairness of state court proceedings.

It was not until 1923 that the Supreme Court finally applied the Fourteenth Amendment's Due Process Clause to reverse state capital convictions of Black men obtained in a courtroom dominated by an angry white mob.[9] The charges against the 'Elaine 12' arose from what has been called the worst race riot in American history. About a hundred Black men in Elaine, Arkansas, mostly sharecroppers, had been holding a meeting in their church to discuss how they might get fairer prices for their cotton crops. Local white men, at least one of whom may have been involved with local law enforcement, arrived to monitor the meeting and fired shots into the church. The situation was tense and, although it is not clear who shot first, shots exchanged outside the church resulted in the death of a white man. Hundreds of white citizens, including Ku Klux Klan members and federal troops, responded to what was being characterized as a Black 'insurrection' by hunting and massacring hundreds of Black men, women, and children. Five white men were also killed. Hundreds of Black men were indiscriminately jailed and tortured to manufacture incriminating evidence for prosecutors to use. The state indicted 122 Black men – and no whites – charging 73 of them with murder.

The habeas corpus appeal the Supreme Court agreed to hear involved six of the Elaine 12, including Frank Moore, who were convicted of murder – despite the fact that there was no credible evidence that these individuals were actually responsible,[10] and despite the fact that it was at least possible that the man in question had accidentally been killed by another white man. A lynch mob was averted only by the promise that those found guilty would be executed 'in the form of law.' White mobs then set out to assure that there would indeed be convictions. 'The Court and neighborhood were thronged with an adverse crowd that threatened

---

[9]   Moore v. Dempsey, 261 U.S. 86 (1923).
[10] The state's 'evidence' was obtained by whipping and torturing Black men until they agreed to say whatever was demanded.

the most dangerous consequences to anyone interfering with the desired result,' in the words of Justice Oliver Wendell Holmes. The trial took 45 minutes; the all-white jury delivered guilty verdicts in about five minutes. When neither the Arkansas state courts nor Governor were willing to set aside these peremptory death sentences, Moore and five other defendants, with the help of the NAACP, brought their case to federal court in a habeas corpus proceeding. Reversing the convictions, Holmes wrote for a six-Justice majority. '[I]f the case is that the whole proceeding is a mask – that counsel, jury and judge were swept to the fatal end by an irresistible wave of public passion,' and the State of Arkansas failed to provide redress, he said, it was the duty of the Supreme Court to intervene as guarantor of the petitioners' constitutional rights.[11] Though not as well-known as the later Scottsboro cases, *Moore v. Dempsey* represented a shift in the Supreme Court's perception of its role and the role of the lower federal courts as a forum for review of state court injustices.

During the next few decades there were several other occasions where the Court reversed shockingly unfair state convictions on the basis of the Due Process Clause. In the notorious cases involving the so-called Scottsboro Boys,[12] for example, the Court reversed Alabama capital convictions on more than one occasion – first because the accused had been assigned a lawyer who did little to prepare for trial and was wholly ineffective,[13] and then because of blatant discrimination in the selection of all-white juries.[14] Despite the disintegration of the state's evidence – one of the two complainants recanted her testimony, admitting the charges were false – no juror at any of the retrials voted to acquit.

It was not until the 1960s that the Warren Court began a due process revolution aimed at containing the influence of racism on criminal proceedings, especially in the southern states.[15] As described in Section 4.1,

---

[11] The six *Moore* defendants were set free, and the NAACP helped them to leave the state of Arkansas to avoid being lynched.

[12] The Scottsboro defendants were nine Black teenagers charged with raping two white women on a train, on the basis of spurious evidence. Dan T. Carter, *Scottsboro: A Tragedy of the American South* (Baton Rouge, LA: Louisiana State University Press, 1969).

[13] Powell v. Alabama, 287 U.S. 45 (1932).

[14] Norris v. Alabama, 294 U.S. 587 (1935).

[15] Burt Neuborne, The Gravitational Pull of Race on the Warren Court (2010) 1 *The Supreme Court Review* 59.

the Court applied most Bill of Rights procedural protections to the states, setting consistent norms for criminal procedure in both federal and state courts. Federal standards came to govern pretrial conduct, including interrogation and identification procedures, as well as court proceedings. The 1960s' Court was willing to play a counter-majoritarian role on behalf of criminal suspects and defendants, mandating an exclusionary rule to enforce the Fourth Amendment;[16] *Miranda* warnings to inform suspects of their right to remain silent during custodial interrogation;[17] constitutionally based safeguards against misidentification in line-ups and other identification proceedings;[18] rights for prisoners;[19] and robust habeas corpus law inviting incarcerated people to bring to federal court claims that their state convictions had been unconstitutional. In the early 1970s, the Court even found the death penalty to be unconstitutional, for a period of a few years.[20]

But as in areas of civil liberties previously discussed, the changing composition of the Court led to backlash: reinstatement of the death penalty a few years later;[21] myriad exceptions to the exclusionary rule and *Miranda*; weakening the protections against mistaken identification; exceptions to the writ of habeas corpus;[22] and reduced sympathy for the plight of prisoners.[23] Only in a few jurisdictions has state law preserved anything like the level of protection against unjust conviction the Warren Court had set.

---

[16]   Mapp v. Ohio, 367 U.S. 643 (1961).

[17]   Miranda v. Arizona, 384 U.S. 436 (1966).

[18]   United States v. Wade, 388 U.S. 218 (1967).

[19]   The rights recognized included procedural due process, access to the courts, and freedom from cruel and unusual punishment. Michael B. Mushlin, *Rights of Prisoners* (Deerfield IL: Clark Boardman Callaghan, 2017–2021).

[20]   Furman v. Georgia, 408 U.S. 238 (1972).

[21]   Gregg v. Georgia, 428 U.S. 153 (1976).

[22]   Stone v. Powell, 428 U.S. 465 (1976), for example, barred federal courts from considering Fourth Amendment exclusionary rule claims in habeas corpus proceedings. Congress also dramatically limited availability of the writ in the 1996 Antiterrorism and Effective Death Penalty Act.

[23]   Susan N. Herman, Slashing and Burning Prisoners' Rights: Congress and the Supreme Court in Dialogue (1998) 77 *Oregon Law Review* 1229.

10 Privacy, autonomy, and family rights

During the 1910s and 1920s, questions about the propriety of using contraceptives manifested themselves in battles over freedom of speech. Margaret Sanger, founder of the organization that became Planned Parenthood, faced prosecution for her pamphlets and speeches advocating birth control. Federal and state 'Comstock laws' declared information about birth control to be the equivalent of obscenity – a topic considered to be, like obscenity, outside the bounds of decency. Civil libertarians defended Sanger's right to advocate for birth control before developing the position that the right to use birth control should itself be considered a fundamental right.[1]

The American eugenics movement, which peaked in the 1920s and 1930s, raised questions about the right to reproductive freedom itself. Eugenics advocates maintained that it was possible to eliminate undesirable human traits – like low intelligence, insanity, and criminality – by selective breeding. The now infamous 1925 case of *Buck v. Bell*[2] found that the practice of negative eugenics, including forced sterilization, was not inconsistent with the US Constitution's guarantee of liberty. Carrie Buck had been sterilized pursuant to a Virginia state law that provided for the involuntary sterilization of people in state institutions who were 'found to be afflicted with an hereditary form of insanity or imbecility.' Justice Oliver Wendell Holmes, a civil liberties defender in other respects, championed the supposed science rather than reproductive freedom. 'It is better for all the world, if instead of waiting to execute degenerate offspring for crime, or to let them starve for their imbecility, society can prevent those who

---

[1]   Leigh Ann Wheeler, *How Sex Became a Civil Liberty* (New York: Oxford University Press, 2014).

[2]   Buck v. Bell, 274 U.S. 200 (1925).

are manifestly unfit from continuing their kind ... Three generations of imbeciles are enough.' Carrie Buck was one of almost 60,000 people sterilized on this theory.

In 1942, while the world could observe the consequences of the Nazi Party's embrace of eugenics, the Supreme Court changed direction, invalidating an Oklahoma statute that called for the sterilization of certain habitual criminals in *Skinner v. Oklahoma*.[3] Without directly attacking the scientific basis of eugenics, Justice William Douglas's majority opinion emphasized the importance of the individual's right to choose to have children – 'We are dealing here with legislation which involves one of the basic civil rights of man' – as well as the tendency of sterilization laws to target marginalized and vulnerable people. 'In evil or reckless hands [the power to sterilize] can cause races or types which are inimical to the dominant group to wither and disappear.' After the eugenics movement had lost its grip on the American imagination, Carrie Buck was found to be of normal intelligence.

During the 1920s, alongside the *Buck v. Bell* decision, the Court ruled that governmental intrusions on family decisions about educating their children were unconstitutional deprivations of the substantive liberty guaranteed by the Due Process Clause.[4]

Later in the twentieth century, building on these 1920s' substantive due process cases and *Skinner*, the Supreme Court endorsed the view that the US Constitution guarantees a 'zone of privacy' where individuals have a fundamental right to make decisions about their personal lives without undue state interference. This zone of privacy – more aptly denominated a zone of autonomy – was said to include one's decisions about family relationships, child-rearing and education, and procreation.

The decision to treat these particular liberties as fundamental rights, which gives the courts the power to strictly scrutinize state laws restricting individual choices in these areas, has been highly controversial. The fact that

---

[3]   Skinner v. Oklahoma, 316 U.S. 535 (1942).
[4]   Meyer v. Nebraska, 262 U.S. 390 (1923) (finding unconstitutional a state statute prohibiting the teaching of the German language); Pierce v. Society of Sisters, 268 U.S. 510 (1925) (finding a state law requiring children to attend public school to deny a constitutional liberty to send one's children to a religious school).

privacy and autonomy rights are not explicitly listed in the Constitution matters to some judges more than to others. Strict constructionists argue that the courts may not legitimately give special protection to unenumerated, implied rights because the Constitution, through its silence on these matters, left it to the states to decide whether to recognize the marriage of a same-sex couple or ban contraceptives or abortion. Those favoring judicial protection of this type of implied fundamental right argue that such intimate decisions are of similar order and magnitude to the rights explicitly protected in the Bill of Rights and should not be subject to the vagaries of state politics.

In 1965, in the landmark case of *Griswold v. Connecticut*,[5] a seven Justice majority of the Court found a Connecticut statute banning the use of contraceptives unconstitutional. In explaining why the decision to use contraceptives should be reserved to individuals rather than subject to state prohibition, Justice Douglas, writing the opinion of the Court, stressed the similarity of decisions taking place in a marital bedroom to the range of privacy rights explicitly protected in the Bill of Rights: the Fourth Amendment's protection against unreasonable searches and seizures; the Third Amendment's ban on quartering soldiers in people's homes; the Fifth Amendment's protection of the private enclave of the mind in the privilege against self-incrimination; and the First Amendment right to freedom of association. The listed rights should not be regarded, said Douglas, as discrete atomistic protections, but as creating a 'penumbra' of rights establishing boundaries in the relationship between individuals and the state – like Brandeis's right to be let alone (see Section 8.3).

Other Justices concurring in *Griswold* relied on American tradition in finding that the state should not be allowed to criminalize the use of contraceptives by a married couple, or on the Constitution's Ninth Amendment, which states that '[t]he enumeration in the Constitution, of certain rights, shall not be construed to deny or disparage others retained by the people.'[6] Concurring Justice Arthur Goldberg referred to the state's ban as a 'totalitarian limitation of family size,' which he saw as being 'at

---

[5]   Griswold v. Connecticut, 381 U.S. 479 (1965).

[6]   People often express surprise that the Ninth Amendment is not cited more often in discussion of implied fundamental rights. This may be attributed to the fact that the actual meaning and intent of the Ninth Amendment have been contested by historians.

complete variance with our constitutional concepts.' If there is no constitutional constraint on a state banning the use of contraceptives, what would then stop a state, asked Goldberg, from decreeing that all husbands and wives must be sterilized after having two children?

Can a right not to have the state coopt individual decisions about marriage and family properly be said to be inherent in American 'constitutional concepts' if that right is not enumerated in the Bill of Rights? The failure to mention reproductive freedom does not show that the framers rejected the fundamentality of this right. After all, the list of rights in the eighteenth-century Bill of Rights was intended only to limit the federal government. Before the expansion of federal power in the mid-twentieth century, it probably would have been unimaginable to anyone that the *federal* government might attempt to regulate marriage or procreation. Any such regulation at that time would have been considered to be purely a matter of state policy, and therefore beyond the reach of the US Constitution. It must also be noted that the framers of the Constitution – the original Constitution, the Bill of Rights, and the Fourteenth Amendment – were all men, operating in a world where women did not have a right to vote and were not regarded as fully citizens. Reproductive freedom might well have seemed to them to be less important, and less interrelated with political life, than it might seem to women, whose bodies and ability to participate in any kind of life beyond their families are at stake. Interpreting rights as circumscribed by the framers' attitudes to women consigns women to being a permanent underclass.

Griswold and most other cases on reproductive freedom have not focused on the perspectives of the people who were excluded from creation of the Constitution, either women or people of color. Michele Goodwin argues that there is a specific basis for finding that the Fourteenth Amendment covers reproductive freedom as a fundamental liberty: some of the abolitionist men who wrote the Thirteenth and Fourteenth Amendments intended to reverse the total denial of reproductive freedom to enslaved Black women, which included condoning systematic rape and destroying their families through sale of their children.[7] The Reconstruction Amendments, she argues, have generally been interpreted as addressing

---

[7]   Michele Goodwin, No, Justice Alito, Reproductive Justice Is in the Constitution (*New York Times*, June 26, 2022). Her argument was in response to the originalist arguments in the *Dobbs* case, see Section 10.4.

the concerns of Black men, erasing the unique experiences of Black women.

10.1 Marriage

Griswold posited that the precincts of the marital bedroom were 'sacred' because marriage is a noble 'association that promotes a way of life, not causes.' The Court would later confront the question of what role the state would be permitted to play in deciding who could get married. Because respect for marriage is indeed an American tradition, state laws limiting the freedom to marry have tended to fall along the fault lines of American democracy, like class, race, and minority sexual orientation. State legislatures agreeing that marriage was sacred were all too willing to limit the ability of people to marry if the state disapproved of the people involved or of their marriage choices.

Following *Griswold*, the Supreme Court struck down various kinds of limitations on marriage, ruling that a state could not make exceptions to the individual freedom to marry without demonstrating a compelling need to do so. For example, the state of Wisconsin prohibited fathers who were behind on child support payments from marrying again without court approval. The Court found that limitation too great a burden on the individual's right to marry.[8] Also invalidated was a Missouri regulation forbidding prisoners from marrying unless the warden of their prison granted them permission based on a finding that the marriage was justified by 'compelling circumstances.'[9] The Court found that this prohibition could not even satisfy the deferential rational basis test applied to most prisoners' rights claims. Ironically, although the inmate plaintiff gained the right to marry another inmate, in the same case the Court found that he did not have a right under the First Amendment to correspond with her.

This split decision shows how seriously the Court has taken state restrictions on the right of particular individuals to marry. But the Court's enthusiasm for the institution of marriage did not immediately lead it to

---

[8] Zablocki v. Redhail, 434 U.S. 374 (1978).
[9] Turner v. Safley, 482 U.S. 78 (1987).

invalidate limitations on the right to marry someone of a different race or the same sex.

Among the many painful legacies of race-based slavery were state 'miscegenation' laws prohibiting interracial marriage. It may seem surprising that it was not until 1967 that the Supreme Court found these laws unconstitutional. The Court had an opportunity in 1955 to review Virginia's anti-miscegenation statute, but declined to take the case,[10] perhaps because it seemed too soon after the previous year's edict in *Brown v. Board of Education*[11] asserting federal court power to integrate public schools, which was still provoking anger and resistance in some regions. But by the 1960s, the Court was ready to issue a strong statement discrediting these racist laws. The aptly named couple in *Loving v. Virginia* had been forced to leave their home because they were deemed to be committing a crime merely by living in Virginia as a married couple.[12] After years of exile, they wanted to return home. Virginia argued that its miscegenation statute did not constitute racial discrimination because it applied equally to people of any race. But Chief Justice Earl Warren found the statute to be both a form of invidious racial discrimination and a denial of the fundamental freedom to marry, which he described as 'one of the "basic civil rights of man," fundamental to our very existence and survival.'

The idea that marriage is an institution of transcendent importance and central to the human condition later also provided the Court with a basis for eventually requiring states to make marriage available to same-sex couples.[13] On this issue too, the Court had had an earlier opportunity to consider the constitutional issue raised. In 1972, the Court entertained the challenge of two men to a Minnesota statute allowing only a man and a woman to marry and ruled that there was no federal question presented in the case. Over 40 years later, in the 2015 case of *Obergefell v. Hodges*, the Court decided that there was not only a federal question, but a fundamental right involved. Justice Anthony Kennedy's opinion shifted from the privacy rationale of *Griswold*, announcing that the right to personal choice regarding marriage is inherent in the concept of individual autonomy. As in *Griswold*, as in *Brown*, as in the incorporation cases, the Court

---

[10]   Naim v. Naim, 350 U.S. 985 (1956).
[11]   Brown v. Board of Education, 347 U.S. 483 (1954).
[12]   Loving v. Virginia, 388 U.S. 1 (1967).
[13]   Obergefell v. Hodges, 576 U.S. 644 (2015).

was requiring recalcitrant states to conform to contemporary national norms.

Obergefell continued the Court's battle over whether unenumerated rights can be deemed fundamental, as well as how to use history. The state defendants as well as the three dissenting Justices emphasized that American history and tradition defined marriage as open only to a man and a woman. But the majority found that eighteenth- and nineteenth-century history was less relevant than the fact that views toward same-sex marriage had recently been evolving. By the time *Obergefell* was decided in 2015, only a minority of states still forbade same-sex marriage. Due to the multi-year strategic campaign of many organizations and individuals, most states had changed their policies through legislation or litigation. The 2015 majority thought this trend showed an evolution in public understanding of fundamental American values that should trigger evolving constitutional protections – as in *Olmstead*. The relevant history was not whether or not American law had accepted same-sex marriage in 1868, when the Fourteenth Amendment was adopted, but whether Americans had come to a new understanding of what the rights of autonomy and dignity should mean in a democracy.

That Americans' views of same sex marriage had indeed evolved was confirmed by the enactment at the end of 2022 of the federal Respect for Marriage Act. Responding to Justice Clarence Thomas's warning in his concurrence in the Dobbs case, see Section 10.4, that unenumerated rights other than abortion might be on the Court's chopping block, Congress took preemptive action, with some bipartisan support, to safeguard marriage equality. While the Act does not require states to offer marriage to same sex couples, it does require states to honor same sex marriages authorized by other states, and rescinds the discriminatory 1996 "Defense of Marriage Act." It is encouraging that, even though the pendulum continues to swing with respect to rights like abortion, progress in the battle against homophobia remains steady.

10.2   Family and living arrangements

The level of generality in interpreting American tradition has been a central issue in determining whether individual life-style decisions other than the decision to marry will also be safeguarded against state interference.

One way in which local governments intrude on decisions about living arrangements is through zoning laws. It is common for zoning laws to designate some districts as restricted to single family homes – as opposed to multiple dwellings – and then to define what constitutes a 'family.' In 1974, the Supreme Court considered the constitutionality of a zoning ordinance that defined a family, for zoning purposes, as comprising not more than two persons unrelated by blood, marriage, or adoption. This restriction on who could share a house in the Village of Belle Terre, New York, was challenged by six unrelated graduate students attending a nearby university, who were surprised to discover that they were committing a crime by sharing a house.[14] The Court decided that there was no fundamental constitutional right to live with unrelated individuals and so the Village could exclude non-families by pointing to any conceivable legitimate interest – like the possibility that unrelated housemates might have noisy parties or contribute to parking problems. It did not matter whether or not those dangers were real, or that offensive conduct could have been more directly addressed by laws that did not restrict individual choices about living arrangements.[15]

By way of contrast, when the City of East Cleveland limited occupancy of a dwelling unit to a single family and defined 'family' as including only a few categories of related individuals, the Supreme Court decided that the city could not constitutionally prohibit a grandmother from living with her son and her two grandsons. The Court explained that this case was entirely different from the *Belle Terre* case because grandmothers are blood relations. The Constitution protects 'the sanctity of the family precisely because the institution of the family is deeply rooted in the Nation's history and traditions,' the Court said, a tradition that is not limited to the nuclear family. 'The tradition of uncles, aunts, cousins, and especially grandparents sharing a household along with parents and children has roots equally venerable and equally deserving of constitutional recognition.'[16]

---

[14]   Each day of violation of the zoning ordinance was considered a separate offense of disorderly conduct under New York state law.
[15]   Village of Belle Terre v. Boraas, 416 U.S. 1 (1974).
[16]   Moore v. City of East Cleveland, 431 U.S. 494 (1977).

As was the case in *Obergefell*, the Court might have emphasized the fundamentality of the decision about one's living arrangements, whether one chooses to live with relatives or not, as essential to the pursuit of happiness. The focus on a constricted view of American tradition as defining which choices are protected and which are not perpetuates the majority's traditional choices, leaving people with non-conforming lifestyles at the mercy of their neighbors. In *Belle Terre*, unlike the contraceptive and marriage cases, the Court did not fulfill its counter-majoritarian mission.

10.3   Private sexual activity

After the decision in *Griswold* to afford special constitutional protection to the intimacy of the marital bedroom, another question that arose was whether intimate activities in the bedrooms of people who were not married would also be protected. This question was especially urgent to LGBTQ people who, at the time, did not even have the option of choosing to marry someone who was not deemed a member of the opposite sex.

Concurring Justice John Marshall Harlan had opined in *Griswold* that because the Court's decision in that case had been based on the American tradition of respecting legally married couples, the right of privacy would not invalidate traditional statutes providing marriage with a legal monopoly on sex by criminalizing adultery, incest, fornication, and consensual sodomy. The first time the Court was asked to find a state consensual sodomy statute unconstitutional, in 1986, a majority of the Court agreed with Harlan and dismissively characterized as 'facetious' plaintiff Michael Hardwick's claim that his non-marital, same-sex sexual activity should also be protected by the right of privacy.[17] Taking a narrow approach in interpreting the relevant tradition, the Court announced that the family rights the Court had protected in other cases bore no resemblance to 'the claimed constitutional right of homosexuals to engage in acts of sodomy.' There was no connection, the majority said, between family, marriage, and procreation on the one hand, and 'homosexual activity' on the other. The Court traced what it declared to be a tradition of forbidding the crime against nature back through common law all the way back to the Bible.

---

[17]   Bowers v. Hardwick, 478 U.S. 186 (1986).

Consensual sodomy laws were rarely enforced, but the existence of those laws created opportunities for the harassment of LGBTQ people. Michael Hardwick, for example, was arrested for consensual sodomy by an officer who entered his bedroom in order to serve him with an invalid arrest warrant for a charge of public drunkenness. Although the state of Georgia dropped the consensual sodomy charge against him, Hardwick decided to bring a civil action to challenge the law. Years later, John Lawrence and Tyron Gardner, an interracial couple, also had the experience of having a police officer enter their bedroom, in Houston, Texas – in their case because someone had falsely complained about a weapons disturbance in the apartment. Texas prosecuted Lawrence and Garner for 'deviate sex' even though the facts underlying that charge were questionable.

The Supreme Court agreed to hear Lawrence and Garner's appeal of the convictions that resulted. Only 17 years after *Bowers v. Hardwick*, the Court resoundingly overruled that case, branding it as a decision that had always been wrong. Justice Anthony Kennedy wrote the majority opinion in *Lawrence v. Texas*,[18] finding the Texas statute prohibiting consensual sodomy to be inconsistent with the Constitution's promise of liberty. Like the ban on use of contraceptives in *Griswold*, this statute raised the specter of police enforcing the law by intruding into people's most private sanctuaries, their bedrooms. But Kennedy portrayed the issue in the case as being about more than just the privacy of the bedroom. At stake was 'liberty in both its spatial and in its more transcendent dimensions.' Kennedy's opinion's focus on autonomy – the right of individuals to make decisions about their personal lives – paved the way for his later opinion in *Obergefell* championing same-sex marriage. As in that case, he portrayed recent history as being more relevant than ancient or nineteenth-century history in deciding what freedoms must be respected. By the time *Lawrence* was decided, only 13 states still retained consensual sodomy laws and those laws were rarely enforced against consenting adults having sex in private. As in the earlier case of *Griswold* and the later case of *Obergefell*, the Court was creating uniformity among the states on an issue where there was already a great deal of consensus.

But the Court has not had occasion to decide whether to extend protection for private sexual conduct to the other categories Harlan thought were distinguishable from *Griswold*, like laws proscribing adultery, fornication

---

[18]   Lawrence v. Texas, 539 U.S. 558 (2003).

(sexual activity outside marriage), and incest.[19] After *Lawrence*, 18 states retained adultery statutes on their books and six had fornication statutes. Those statutes are rarely enforced so challenges to their constitutionality do not arise. In the years after *Obergefell*, some state legislatures decided to remove adultery and fornication statutes from their books.

These actions are a reminder that state legislatures can sometimes be more protective of civil liberties than the courts force them to be. State courts have also been active in protecting private sexual conduct. In 1998 – years before the Supreme Court's decision in *Lawrence* – Georgia became the fifth state to reject the sanctimony of *Bowers v. Hardwick* when the state supreme court found that the statute the Supreme Court had upheld in that case was unconstitutional under the Georgia state constitution.[20] But even after court rulings, legislatures may resist results they have not voluntarily chosen. After *Loving*, for example, a number of states left anti-miscegenation statutes on their books because legislators were unwilling to take the risk that people in their state might be offended by the Court's decision. And in the area of abortion, states like Texas defied long-standing Supreme Court law by enacting flatly inconsistent statutes in an effort to avoid or change federal constitutional law.

10.4 Abortion

Abortion has been an explosively divisive issue in American courts and legislatures, pitting an ardent belief that a pregnant person should have a right to terminate a pregnancy against an equally ardent belief that a fetus is an unborn person entitled to protection.

Under English law and in colonial America, abortion was legal before quickening, the point at which fetal movement can be felt (usually after about 15–20 weeks of pregnancy). During the nineteenth century, state laws began to ban abortion even before quickening and by 1910, all states had criminal abortion laws, with varying exceptions such as

---

[19]   The Supreme Court upheld a ban on polygamy long ago and has not revisited the issue. Reynolds v. United States, 98 U.S. 145 (1879), discussed in Section 7.1.
[20]   Powell v. State, 510 S.E.2d 18 (1998).

medical emergency. Historians have offered various explanations for the adoption of these Victorian era laws, including the sexist reaction of the male medical profession to women practitioners and homeopaths who provided abortifacients, and growing alarm about women portraying voluntary motherhood as part of their movement toward political equality.

Criminalizing abortion created substantial new health risks. Affluent women were often able to secure safe abortions through money and travel, but thousands of less affluent women experienced health problems or died each year due to botched illegal abortions or self-abortions. During the 1960s, women and their allies organized, lobbied, and litigated to change abortion laws, with an image of a coat hanger as the grim symbol of extra-legal abortion. Some states liberalized their abortion laws, but more than half the states, including Texas, seemed unlikely to modify their laws unless the federal courts forced them to do so.

In 1973, the Supreme Court in the now iconic case of *Roe v. Wade*[21] did just that, invalidating the Texas statute criminalizing abortion on the ground that women[22] in every state had a fundamental Fourteenth Amendment right to choose to have an abortion. That conclusion was portrayed as within the zone of privacy recognized in cases like *Griswold*, empowering individuals to make their own decisions about their bodies, their families, and their lives.

While the decision was fairly well received at the time, Justice Harry Blackmun's majority opinion in *Roe v. Wade* was criticized as sounding like a legislative compromise. It was indeed a compromise, offering something to everyone. Blackmun balanced the competing arguments rather than awarding total victory to one side or the other. His opinion announced that fetuses do not have constitutional rights, but that the state has an interest in the potential life of the fetus that becomes compelling at the point of viability, when the fetus is capable of sustaining life outside the womb (about 24 to 26 weeks). Therefore states would be permitted to regulate or ban abortion after viability, at about the end of the second tri-

---

[21]   Roe v. Wade, 410 U.S. 113 (1973).

[22]   Neither *Roe* nor later cases noted that not all pregnant persons are women. The politics of abortion have been so closely tied to women's equality that it is not always inappropriate to refer to abortion as a right of women, while acknowledging that a transgender man may also be pregnant.

mester. Recognizing that states were likely to use spurious health regulations to prevent the exercise of a right that was now guaranteed in theory, Blackmun drew a line between the first and second trimesters, declaring that states could enact measures reasonably related to health during the second trimester, but during the first trimester had to leave decisions to a woman and her doctor.

Over time, the backlash to *Roe v. Wade* grew. Defiant states enacted over 1,000 intimidating and burdensome regulations – elaborate informed consent requirements followed by waiting periods, parental and spousal notice or consent requirements, ultrasound requirements, targeted regulations of abortion providers – aimed at preventing or dissuading pregnant people from obtaining abortions. Republicans saw an opportunity to wrest Catholic voters who disapproved of abortion away from the Democratic Party; President Ronald Reagan promised to appoint five Supreme Court Justices who would overrule *Roe v. Wade*. As the years passed and the composition of the Supreme Court changed, the seven-Justice majority in *Roe v. Wade* dwindled. During the 1970s and 1980s, the Court continued to invalidate some state restrictions not reasonably related to health, but by a decreasing margin, and upheld other kinds of restrictions, including bans on the use of public money to fund abortions.

By 1992, when a case concerning the constitutionality of Pennsylvania abortion regulations arrived at the Court, four of the Justices were Reagan appointees. Only one Justice was a Democratic appointee: Byron White, who had been one of the two dissenters in *Roe v. Wade*. But in *Planned Parenthood of Southeastern Pennsylvania v. Casey*[23] two of Reagan's appointees – Sandra Day O'Connor and Anthony Kennedy – joined by three other Justices, invoked the doctrine of *stare decisis* and declined to overrule what they saw as the 'essential core' of *Roe v. Wade*: (1) the recognition of a fundamental right; (2) the prohibition on banning abortion pre-viability; and (3) inclusion of a health exception.[24]

---

[23]   Planned Parenthood of Southeastern Pennsylvania v. Casey, 505 U.S. 833 (1992).

[24]   At the same time the Court jettisoned the trimester framework and substituted an 'undue burden' test.

The plurality opinion identified four factors as relevant in any *stare decisis* analysis, in what came to be known as the precedent on precedent:

> whether *Roe*'s central rule has been found unworkable; whether the rule's limitation on state power could be removed without serious inequity to those who have relied upon it or significant damage to the stability of the society governed by it; whether the law's growth in the intervening years has left *Roe*'s central rule a doctrinal anachronism discounted by society; and whether *Roe*'s premises of fact have so far changed in the ensuing two decades as to render its central holding somehow irrelevant or unjustifiable in dealing with the issue it addresses.

Justice O'Connor extolled the principle of *stare decisis* as critical to constraining the power of individual judges to shape the law according to their own personal and political predilections. Without a strong reason for overturning previous law, as defined in the four factors, she believed that Justices should respect the work of the Court as a whole even if they did not agree with a particular decision. Four Justices dissented, arguing that *Roe v. Wade* should be overruled because whether a decision is wrong is more important than whether it is settled law.

The *Casey* compromise survived for 30 years. But as Roger Baldwin observed, no civil liberties battle stays won.

By 2020, President Donald Trump had succeeded in appointing three very conservative Justices, one of whom replaced women's rights champion Ruth Bader Ginsburg. The reconstituted Court wasted little time in dramatically overruling *Roe v. Wade* in a 2022 Mississippi case, *Dobbs v. Jackson Women's Health Organization*.[25] Justice Samuel Alito, writing for five Justices,[26] gave two reasons for finding that there is no constitutional right to have an abortion: that there was no right to abortion explicitly listed in the Constitution; and that American history and tradition did not recognize any such right before *Roe*. Alito thought it critical that state legislatures had opposed abortion in the late nineteenth century, when the Fourteenth Amendment was adopted. His originalist judicial philosophy,

---

[25]   Dobbs v. Jackson Women's Health Organization, 597 U.S. ___ (2022).

[26]   Chief Justice Roberts concurred only in the judgment, contending that because of *stare decisis* the Court should have proceeded incrementally and upheld the Mississippi law banning abortion after 15 weeks without wholly overruling *Roe v. Wade*. His more cautious vote was no longer decisive.

rooted in the past, rejected outright the idea that the meaning of the Constitution can and should evolve.

Almost half a century after *Roe* nationalized the right to choose, the Court declared that it would remain neutral on the relative importance of control of reproductive decisions and the respect due a fetus, returning the issue to the vagaries of state politics.

The three dissenters argued that nothing relevant had changed since the Court had confronted the same arguments in *Planned Parenthood v. Casey* and decided to preserve the precedent of *Roe v. Wade* – except the composition of the Court. The majority responded by characterizing *stare decisis* as not being 'an inexorable command,' and underscored its willingness to disregard precedent by diverging from the 1992 Court's *stare decisis* analysis itself.[27] The 2022 majority's version of relevant factors heavily weighted the Justices' disagreement with the *Roe v. Wade* opinion rather than the decision's status as a settled precedent. *Roe v. Wade*, Alito declared, was 'egregiously wrong' and 'exceptionally weak' in its reasoning.

As to the *stare decisis* factors the *Casey* Court had identified, the majority contended that it should not matter whether premises of fact or intervening law had undermined a case's holding, because a decision that is wrong is wrong regardless of whether or not anything changes subsequent to the decision. The dissenters reiterated *Casey*'s conclusion that for almost half a century, women had relied on *Roe v. Wade*, even in its weakened form, to allow them to act as full members of society by controlling their lives. The majority had little to say about the impact the decision would actually have on women, remarking that pregnancy is often unexpected, and that reliance interests are most pertinent in commercial and property disputes. In this reformulation, *stare decisis* loses power as a stabilizing force holding settled law above individual judges' preferences.

In support of their reversal of *Roe*, the majority pointed approvingly to earlier cases where long-standing precedents had been overruled – like *Brown v. Board of Education* reversing a half century of case law uphold-

---

[27] Alito used a reformulation he had adopted in Janus v. AFSCME, 585 U.S. ___ (2018) to justify overruling a 1977 decision that requiring public sector employees to pay some union fees did not violate the First Amendment.

ing racial apartheid. But those admirable cases were generally instances in which a later Court expanded rights or equality. *Dobbs* was the first case in Supreme Court history where the Court overruled a precedent declaring a fundamental right.

A number of state legislatures, including Mississippi, had defied *Roe* and *Casey* by banning pre-viability abortions before the decision in *Dobbs*. Some states had enacted repressive abortion statutes ready to be triggered by a decision like *Dobbs*; a few states had archaic anti-abortion laws they had not updated while *Roe* and *Casey* were the law. In sum, *Dobbs* was expected to lead to about half the states banning or severely restricting abortion, often not allowing any exception for cases of rape or incest, or for some abortions necessary for health reasons. Battle lines were drawn between states hostile to abortion and states that retained a right to abortion under their own laws. Some states sought to prevent their residents from traveling to another state in order to get an abortion, a move of questionable constitutionality. *Dobbs* also fueled support in some states for laws criminalizing pregnant people for having an abortion, for aggressive investigation of miscarriages, and generally policing the womb.[28] State anti-abortion laws were expected to have the greatest negative impact on the least affluent and least powerful, including minorities.

Meanwhile, Texas had tried self-help to neutralize *Roe v. Wade* rather than waiting for the Court to change its mind. The legislature passed a law prohibiting doctors from performing an abortion after a fetal heartbeat could be detected (about six weeks) and sought to immunize the law from federal court review by prohibiting state officials from enforcing it. Instead, the law encouraged private individuals to bring lawsuits against doctors and anyone else who 'performs, induces, assists, or intends to assist' an abortion, promising large rewards (a minimum of $10,000 for prevailing plaintiffs) and asymmetrical litigation advantages. The statute was flatly inconsistent with *Roe v. Wade*, but tried to evade a court ruling enjoining its enforcement by sidelining the state actors who otherwise would have been the defendants in such a lawsuit. The Supreme Court allowed that tactic to work.[29] It remains to be seen whether the Court's toleration of state defiance of federal constitutional rulings in the abortion

---

[28]   Michele Goodwin, *Policing the Womb* (New York: Cambridge University Press, 2020).

[29]   Whole Woman's Health v. Jackson, 595 U.S. ___ (2021).

area will extend to other civil liberties as well, perhaps through procedural maneuvers like the Texas model.

The Court's central justification for its decision in *Dobbs* was that the Court should not interfere in democratic decision-making. People who did not like their state's law, the Court said, should use the political process to lobby or replace their legislators. But the problem with this ostensibly democratic solution is that state legislatures are the least representative elected bodies in the country, because of the power of legislators representing only a minority of voters to retain their seats by manipulating districting and election rules (see Chapter 12). And women, 51 percent of the US population, comprise only about 31 percent of state legislators.

Polls showed that from the time of *Roe* to the time of *Dobbs*, over 60 percent of Americans have supported a right to abortion, at least under some circumstances, and did not want to see *Roe v. Wade* overruled. The rationale for affording the Supreme Court a counter-majoritarian veto was supposed to be to allow the Court to protect unpopular rights. In the *Dobbs* case, the Court was counter-majoritarian in the wrong direction, defying the view of most Americans that a civil liberty should be respected.

At the oral argument in *Dobbs*, Justice Sonia Sotomayor asked, 'Will this institution survive the stench that this creates in the public perception – that the Constitution and its reading are just political acts?' Another key question, posed by Justice Thomas in his concurrence, was what other previously recognized civil liberties the emboldened Court might retract.

11   Rights of Equality

This section will briefly outline some of the key features of US equal protection law.

Section 1.4 described the limited nature of the constitutional version of equality, as compared with more expansive concepts of civil rights and human rights law. The Equal Protection Clause of the Fourteenth Amendment only addresses *state* and not private action denying equal protection of the laws and it is not considered to impose any obligation on the state or federal government to protect people against discrimination of any sort, including official or private acts of violence.

11.1   Suspect classifications and strict scrutiny

As set out in Section 4.1, the famous Footnote 4 launched the suspect classification doctrine, which instructs courts to give strict scrutiny to – and therefore almost always to invalidate – laws or official actions discriminating against a 'discrete and insular minority.' Under this rubric, the courts give strict scrutiny to classifications drawn on the basis of race, religion, ethnicity, national origin, and sometimes citizenship status. Classifications drawn on the basis of gender are considered quasi-suspect, receiving intermediate scrutiny. The Court has never explicitly decided what level of scrutiny should apply to discrimination against LGBTQ people, although several cases have invalidated specific forms of discrimination on the theory that they were grounded in animus, and so did not serve any legitimate purpose.[1]

---

[1]   Romer v. Evans, 517 U.S. 620 (1996). See William D. Araiza, *Animus: A Short Introduction to Bias in the Law* (New York: New York University Press, 2017) for a discussion of this theory.

But this judicial solicitude applies only to explicit or intentional discrimination. In a number of cases, the Supreme Court has held that governmental actions that have a disproportionate impact on the basis of race will not receive strict scrutiny unless it can be shown that those actions were intended to be discriminatory. For example, a civil service test that resulted in people of color being less likely to get positions as police officers was upheld as a well-intentioned effort to field people with good verbal skills.[2] A Georgia death penalty statute that had a racially discriminatory impact was upheld because Georgia only used the statute *despite*, not *because*, of its unequal impact.[3] Challenges to racial profiling, discriminatory arrests, sentencing, or use of force brought on the basis of damning statistics are unlikely to succeed. To have a chance at a favorable judicial ruling, a challenger will have to establish that they personally were intentionally targeted because of their race, or other invidious basis. The Court's decisions show no appreciation of how difficult it is to muster such proof – and simply ignore the problem of unconscious bias.

11.2   School desegregation

In 1954, in *Brown v. Board of Education*,[4] a unanimous Court found that separate but equal public education is an unconstitutional denial of equal protection. That decision, condemning racially segregated schools, has been hailed as one of the Court's greatest accomplishments.

The decision in *Brown* was met with considerable resistance. The federal courts labored for years to integrate schools in areas that had been intentionally segregated.[5] Ironically, schools in the South came to be more integrated than schools in other parts of the country where segregation was an incidental result of factors like demographics rather than a legal mandate and therefore was not constitutionally actionable. But starting in the 1970s, a changing Supreme Court withdrew federal court supervision in districts that had once become 'unitary.' Due to demographic

---

2   Washington v. Davis, 426 U.S. 229 (1976).
3   McCleskey v. Kemp, 481 U.S. 279 (1987).
4   Brown v. Board of Education, 347 U.S. 483 (1954).
5   See Jack Peltason, *Fifty-Eight Lonely Men: Southern Federal Judges and School Desegregation* (Champaign, IL: University of Illinois Press, 1971).

and other factors, many of the schools in those districts reverted to being racially unbalanced. But the Court declared victory, explaining that the goal of *Brown* was not to integrate schools, but merely to end intentional state-sponsored segregation. That construct became the basis for the Court, in the twenty-first century, prohibiting school districts from voluntarily attempting to integrate their schools if their policies paid attention to race.[6]

Thus, the Court redefined the nature of the problem in *Brown*, declaring that what is invidious is not discrimination against a discrete and insular minority, but any governmental classification drawn on the basis of race, no matter who is helped or harmed. Integration was redefined as the absence of intentional segregation rather than as a positive goal. As in many other areas, the Court had ostentatiously forbidden formal discrimination by the state, but failed to address the very real problems of *de facto* racism.

The aftermath of *Brown* led some critics to raise questions about how effective the Supreme Court can be in leading progressive social change.[7] The current Court is not trying to lead but to disable federal and state efforts to promote equality.

11.3   Affirmative action

The decision to treat any race-based classifications as suspect, even if they are part of an affirmative action plan, was said in a 1995 case to be a simple matter of 'consistency.'[8]

In the first decade of the twenty-first century, Justice Sandra Day O'Connor, the deciding vote in affirmative action cases, declared that strict (scrutiny) in theory need not be fatal in fact. She was willing to uphold affirmative action programs serving the purpose of promoting

---

[6]   Parents Involved in Community Schools v. Seattle School Dist. No. 1, 551 U.S. 701 (2007).

[7]   Gerald N. Rosenberg, *The Hollow Hope: Can Courts Bring About Social Change?* (Chicago, IL: University of Chicago Press, 2nd edition, 2008).

[8]   Adarand Constructors, Inc. v. Peña, 515 U.S. 200 (1995).

diversity in higher education, as long as race was only one aspect of a holistic admissions decision.[9] The compromise on affirmative action, allowing some race-conscious programs but not others, held for some time. But by 2022, the Justices who insisted that the best way to get rid of racism is simply to stop paying attention to race had been joined by other Justices who were expected to share those views, leaving affirmative action law in a potential state of flux.[10]

---

[9]   Grutter v. Bollinger, 539 U.S. 306 (2003).

[10] A pair of cases argued in the 2022 Term, Students for Fair Admissions v. President & Fellows of Harvard College, Docket No. 20-1199, and Students for Fair Admissions v. University of North Carolina, Docket No. 21–707, provided an opportunity for the Court to overrule the earlier cases.

12 Rights of democratic participation

It can easily be argued that the rights of democratic participation – to vote, to have one's vote count, to run for office – are the most critical of all civil liberties. As Chief Justice Earl Warren once said, these rights are preservative of all other rights.

As part of the ugly compromise over state's rights and slavery, the eighteenth-century Constitution empowered the states to decide who would be eligible to vote. This was just one manifestation of the Constitution's pattern of conferring electoral power on the states rather than on the people. Each state controls two Senate seats, regardless of its population; each state can decide whether its people or its legislature will choose presidential electors. In combination these powers enable a minority of American voters to control not only state but national decisions.

For the most part, the states exercised their authority to ensure that people who had not been included in the constitutional debates would remain disenfranchised – women, enslaved people, men without sufficient property – even though those groups constituted a majority of a state's population.

In 1870, the Fifteenth Amendment prohibited states from denying the vote on the basis of race, color, or previous condition of servitude.[1] But for the next century, states wanting to keep the vote white employed all kinds

---

[1] Other amendments further democratizing the right to vote came later: the Nineteenth Amendment prohibited states from disenfranchising women in 1920; the Twenty-Fourth Amendment prohibited poll taxes in federal elections in 1964; the Twenty-Sixth Amendment enfranchised people over 18 years in 1971.

of pretexts and subterfuges – including poll taxes and formidable literacy tests – to keep Black people from voting, all without explicitly mentioning race. For example, an 1898 Louisiana law declared that people who were unable to pass the required literacy test would nevertheless be eligible to vote if they owned property or if their grandfather had been entitled to vote. Enslaved people had been forcibly kept illiterate and were not allowed to vote, so within a few years after passage of this grandfather clause, the voter registration of Black men plummeted from 44.8 percent of otherwise eligible men to 4.0 percent. In places where Black people were able to navigate the legal obstacle course, vicious campaigns of fraud, intimidation, and violence aimed to keep them from registering or voting.

Congress, which had been given special enforcement powers under the Fifteenth Amendment, took almost a century to enact a meaningful Voting Rights Act – which it finally did in 1965, inspired by attacks on voting rights demonstrators in Selma, Alabama.

During the 1960s, the Warren Court prioritized promotion of voting rights and equality, taking very seriously its Footnote 4 counter-majoritarian role in representation reinforcement (see Section 4.1). The Court established a 'one man, one vote' rule, for example, to check state attempts at malapportionment (drawing districts so that people have different degrees of voting power).[2] The Court also declared that laws disenfranchising people would be subject to strict scrutiny.[3]

But in later decades, the Supreme Court's attitude to voting rights has shifted dramatically. The Court again allows states freedom to adopt daunting measures – like voter identification requirements, obstacles to voter registration, limitations on early or absentee voting – that although superficially race neutral, have a highly disparate impact on the basis of race.[4] It is not coincidental that creation of disproportionate racial impact aligns with political partisanship. Republican legislators in many states aim to reduce the vote of minority voters they expect would support Democrats, sometime deflecting charges of racism by cheerfully pointing

---

[2] Reynolds v. Sims, 377 U.S. 533 (1964).
[3] Kramer v. Union Free School District No. 15, 395 U.S. 621 (1969).
[4] Carol Anderson, *One Person, No Vote: How Voter Suppression Is Destroying Our Democracy* (New York: Bloomsbury Publishing, 2018).

out that their non-racist purpose in putting a thumb on the scale is simply to win elections. The choices made by Supreme Court Justices in the area of elections have closely aligned with the political party of the president who appointed them, with Republican-appointed Justices currently in the majority more sympathetic to states' rights than to equal voting rights.

The twenty-first century Court is not as deferential to Congress as it is to the states, even though Congress has special enforcement powers under the Fourteenth and Fifteenth Amendments. The Court has eviscerated the landmark Voting Rights Act in two major decisions. The first case arose when Shelby County, Alabama, one of the jurisdictions Congress had identified as needing federal intervention, complained of having to preclear its voting laws with the US Department of Justice. The Court empathized with the indignity Shelby County suffered by being required to 'beseech' the federal government, but not with the thousands of people who would be prevented, discouraged, or deterred from voting by the renaissance of thinly disguised Jim Crow voting laws.[5] Chief Justice Roberts announced that the country had moved on, and that the pre-clearance provisions of the Voting Rights Act might no longer need to apply to Alabama. This holding neutralized the preclearance requirement. Dissenting Justice Ruth Bader Ginsburg compared discarding Congress's protection against a jurisdiction backsliding on the basis that the pro-vision had been successful with 'throwing away your umbrella during a rainstorm because you haven't been getting wet.' The Shelby County decision immediately led to a proliferation of new voter suppression laws. During the following decade, an increasingly conservative Court rewrote another essential provision of the Voting Rights Act, which provided for judicial review of voter suppression laws, thereby disarming all three branches of the federal government.[6]

Furthermore, after decades of debate about whether and how to address extreme partisan gerrymandering, which state legislatures use to lock in the power of an incumbent political party and effectively prevent regime change, the Supreme Court declared it was abandoning the field, ruling that gerrymandering is a political question and should be left to the

---

5   Shelby County v. Holder, 570 U.S. 529 (2013).
6   Brnovich Democratic National Committee, 594 U.S. ___ (2021) found that the Voting Rights Act did not prevent Arizona from undermining the voting power of minorities including Native Americans.

states.[7] This decision allowed the Republican North Carolina legislature to use sophisticated computer programs to divide up the state population algorithmically so that although the state had about half Democratic and half Republican voters, the congressional delegation elected under this carefully drawn map consisted of ten Republicans and three Democrats – but only because, one legislator shamelessly announced, they could not figure out a way to get to 11–2.[8] The North Carolina courts subsequently found the gerrymandered map to violate the state constitution; the Supreme Court countered by agreeing to hear an appeal raising the bold argument that the Supreme Court should interpret the Constitution to allow only the state *legislatures* and not the state courts to make such decisions.[9]

If the Court endorses this 'independent state legislature' doctrine, state courts and executive branches will also be deprived of power to promote fair elections. That would leave unrepresentative state legislatures as the final arbiters of whether regime change is possible, jeopardizing civil liberties and crippling American democracy.

---

[7]   Rucho v. Common Cause, 588 U.S. ___ (2019).

[8]   Democrats have also manipulated district lines, but are prone to laws that facilitate registration and voting because, principle aside, they believe larger turnout of less elite populations will advantage their party.

[9]   Moore v. Harper, Case 21-1271, February 14, 2022. See https://www .supremecourt.gov/docket/docketfiles/html/public/21-1271.html.   Four Justices had previously expressed support for the extreme 'independent state legislature' doctrine, possibly portending another radical change in the law that would maximize the ability of conservative legislators to hold on to their power, even if most of the state's voters disapprove of them.

13 Afterword: The state of US civil liberties

New civil liberties challenges arise all the time – sometimes from emerging technology, sometimes from natural forces. The global pandemic led to intense debate over the acceptability of various forms of governmental control of people's lives, and the treatment of vulnerable populations like prisoners. Our developing understanding of biology has generated urgent issues relating to the rights of transgender people to choose a bathroom, receive gender-affirming health care, or participate in a sports team.

Whether new constitutional rights will be recognized, or previously recognized rights withdrawn, depends largely on the will of the Supreme Court. The Court's current conservative majority, many of whom are young enough to serve for decades to come, takes seriously some libertarian rights, like freedom of speech and religion, and the right to bear arms, but not many others. Politics will determine whether Congress or the states will offer additional protection for civil liberties the Court under-enforces, like reproductive choice, freedom from unreasonable searches and seizures, and equality of justice. But the Supreme Court also has a direct influence over electoral politics, through voting rights jurisprudence that leaves minority voters stranded and seems calculated to entrench libertarian rather than egalitarian values.

Polls showed that following the 2021 Term, an increasing number of Americans regarded the Supreme Court as politically partisan, with only 25 percent of those polled expressing confidence in the Court – a historic low. Apprehension of the Court's outsized power to thwart the values of a majority of Americans sparked national conversations about whether the Supreme Court needs to be reformed. The Constitution does provide political checks against potential Supreme Court tyranny: constitutional amendment to overturn particular decisions; impeachment of individual Justices; and gradual change in the composition of the Court through appointments. But the cumbersome amendment and impeachment processes are rarely used, and attrition is a slow and uncertain process. A commission appointed by Democratic president Joe Biden considered the desirability of effecting changes in the size of the Court, the appointments process, and the terms of service, with an eye to making the Court more representative. But the Commission did not coalesce around any one reform and, in any event, Republican opposition would make reform in any of these directions unlikely.

Many observers have expressed pessimism about the trajectory of American civil liberties and American democracy. The twentieth-century rise of civil liberties was tied to legal liberalism, focused on persuading the courts, mostly the federal courts, to recognize and expand rights. That strategy produced some successes, even if they mostly proved ephemeral. But with the Supreme Court now facing in the other direction on so many issues, the fate of civil liberties depends on finding detours around the federal courts. With the decentralization of debates on issues like abortion, battles must be fought in each individual state rather than in one sweeping Supreme Court case. In some jurisdictions state courts may well continue to preserve and promote civil liberties beyond those the Supreme Court prefers. But in over half the states that avenue is not promising.

It seems that the future of US civil liberties throughout the country will have to depend on strategies other than judicial review – including the contemporary equivalents of the demonstrations, pamphlets, and organizing that the ACLU employed in the 1920s before the courts became civil libertarian.

Only time will tell if the pendulum will swing back.[1]

---

[1]   In one interesting reading of the cycles of American history, legal scholar Jack Balkin suggests that another progressive era could emerge. Jack Balkin, *The Cycles of Constitutional Time* (New York: Oxford University Press, 2020).

Bibliography

ACLU. Picking up the Pieces: Policing in America, a Minneapolis Case Study (2015) https://www.aclu.org/issues/racial-justice/race-and-criminal-justice/picking-pieces?redirect=feature/picking-pieces.

Alexander, James and Stanley N. Katz (eds). *A Brief Narrative on the Case and Trial of John Peter Zenger, Printer of the New York Weekly Journal* (Cambridge, MA: Belknap, 1963).

Anderson, Carol. *One Person, No Vote: How Voter Suppression Is Destroying Our Democracy* (New York: Bloomsbury Publishing, 2018).

Araiza, William D. *Animus: A Short Introduction to Bias in the Law* (New York: New York University Press, 2017).

Aronson, Amy. *Crystal Eastman: A Revolutionary Life* (New York: Oxford University Press, 2019).

Balkin, Jack. *The Cycles of Constitutional Time* (New York: Oxford University Press, 2020).

Beard, Charles. *An Economic Interpretation of the Constitution* (New York: Simon & Schuster, originally published 1913).

Blackstone, William. *Commentaries on the Laws of England* (Oxford: Clarendon Press, 1765–1770).

Blasi, Vincent. The Checking Value in First Amendment Theory (1977) 2(3) *American Bar Foundation Research Journal* 521.

Brannon, Valerie C. *Free Speech and the Regulation of Social Media Content* (Washington, DC: Congressional Research Service, 2019).

Carter, Dan T. *Scottsboro: A Tragedy of the American South* (Baton Rouge, LA: Louisiana State University Press, 1969).

Cole, David. *Enemy Aliens* (New York: New Press, revised edition, 2005).

Cole, David. *Engines of Liberty: The Power of Citizen Activists to Make Constitutional Law* (New York: Basic Books, 2017).

Colorado Jury Awards $14 Million to Demonstrators Injured in George Floyd Protests (New York Times, March 26, 2022) https://www.nytimes.com/2022/03/26/us/denver-george-floyd-protests-ruling.html.

Cose, Ellis. *Democracy, If We Can Keep It: The ACLU's 100-Year Fight for Rights in America* (New York: The New Press, 2020).

Cover, Robert M. The Left, the Right and the First Amendment: 1918–1928 (1981) 40(3) *Maryland Law Review* 349.

Delgado, Richard. Campus Antiracism Rules: Constitutional Narratives in Collision (1990) 85 *Northwestern University Law Review* 343.

Dworkin, Ronald. *Taking Rights Seriously* (Cambridge, MA: Harvard University Press, 1977).

Ely, John Hart. *Democracy and Distrust: A Theory of Judicial Review* (Cambridge, MA: Harvard University Press, 1981).

Felder, Ben. As Critical Race Theory Stirs National Debate, Oklahoma Bill Seeks to Alter Teaching of Slavery (*The Oklahoman*, December 16, 2021) https://www.oklahoman.com/story/news/2021/12/16/critical-race-theory-oklahoma-rep-jim-olsen-bill-teaching-slavery/8912667002/.

Finan, Christopher M. *How Free Speech Saved Democracy: The Untold History of How the First Amendment Became an Essential Tool for Securing Liberty and Social Justice* (Lebanon, NH: Steerforth Press, 2022).

Goodwin, Michele. *Policing the Womb* (New York: Cambridge University Press, 2020).

Goodwin, Michele. No, Justice Alito, Reproductive Justice Is in the Constitution (*New York Times*, June 26, 2022).

Gora, Joel M. Free Speech Matters: The Roberts Court and the First Amendment (2016) 25(1) *Journal of Law and Policy*.

Hasen, Richard L. *Cheap Speech: How Disinformation Poisons Our Politics – and How to Cure It* (New Haven, CT: Yale University Press, 2022).

Herman, Susan N. Slashing and Burning Prisoners' Rights: Congress and the Supreme Court in Dialogue (1998) 77 *Oregon Law Review* 1229.

Herman, Susan N. *The Right to a Speedy and Public Trial* (Westport, CT: Praeger, 3rd edition, 2006).

Herman, Susan N. The USA PATRIOT Act and the Submajoritarian Fourth Amendment (2006) 41 *Harvard Civil Rights-Civil Liberties Law Review* 67.

Herman, Susan N. 'Reading between the Lines: Judicial Protection for Socioeconomic Rights under the South African and United States Constitutions,' in P. Andrews and S. Bazilli (eds), *Comparative Constitutionalism and Rights: Global Perspectives* (Lake Mary, FL: Vandeplas, 2008).

Herman, Susan N. *Taking Liberties: The War on Terror and the Erosion of American Democracy* (New York: Oxford University Press, 2014).

Herman, Susan N. Ab(ju)dication: How Procedure Defeats Civil Liberties in the 'War on Terror' (2017) 50(1) *Suffolk University Law Review* 79.

Hoag, Alexis J. The Color of Justice (2022) April *University of Michigan Law Review*.

Howard, A.E. Dick. *The Road from Runnymede: Magna Carta and Constitutionalism in America* (Charlottesville, VA: University of Virginia Press, 2015).

Irons, Peter. *Justice at War: The Story of the Japanese-American Internment Cases* (Oakland, CA: University of California Press, 1993).

Kalven, Harry, The Metaphysics of the Law of Obscenity (1960) 1 *Supreme Court Review*.

Karlan, Pamela et al. Symposium: The New Countermajoritarian Difficulty (2021) 109(6) *California Law Review*.

Kessler, Jeremy K. The Administrative Origins of Modern Civil Liberties Law (2014) 114 *Columbia Law Review*.

LaFave, Wayne R. *Search and Seizure: A Treatise on the Fourth Amendment* (Eagan, MN: Thomson Reuters West, 6th edition, 2020).

Landynski, Jacob W. *Search and Seizure and the Supreme Court: A Study in Constitutional Interpretation* (Baltimore, MD: Johns Hopkins Press, 1966).

Larson, Carlton F. The Declaration of Independence: A 225th Anniversary Re-Interpretation (2001) 76(3) *Washington Law Review* 701.

Lasson, Nelson B. *The History and Development of the Fourth Amendment to the United States Constitution* (Baltimore, MD: Johns Hopkins Press, 1937).

Lawrence, Charles R. III. The Id, the Ego, and Equal Protection: Reckoning with Unconscious Racism (1987) 39(2) *Stanford Law Review* 317.

Levy, Leonard W. *The Emergence of a Free Press* (New York: Oxford University Press, 1985).

MacKinnon, Catharine. Pornography, Civil Rights, and Speech (1985) 20(1) *Harvard Civil Rights-Civil Liberties Law Review*.

MacKinnon, Catharine. *Toward a Feminist Theory of the State* (Cambridge, MA: Harvard University Press, 1989).

Matsuda, Mari. Public Response to Racist Speech: Considering the Victim's Story (1989) 87(8) *Michigan Law Review* 2320.

Michelman, Frank. On Protecting the Poor Through the Fourteenth Amendment (1969) 83 *Harvard Law Review* 7.

Neuborne, Burt. *The Values of Campaign Finance Reform* (New York: Brennan Center for Justice, 1997).

Neuborne, Burt. The Gravitational Pull of Race on the Warren Court (2010) 1 *The Supreme Court Review* 59.

Neuborne, Burt. *Madison's Music: On Reading the First Amendment* (New York: New Press, 2015).

Packer, Herbert. *The Limits of the Criminal Sanction* (Redwood City, CA: Stanford University Press, 1968).

Polenberg, Richard. *Fighting Faiths: The Abrams Case, the Supreme Court, and Free Speech* (Ithaca, NY: Cornell University Press, 1999).

Rehnquist, William. *All the Laws but One: Civil Liberties in Wartime* (New York: Random House, 1998).

Romero, Anthony and Dina Temple-Raston. *In Defense of Our America: The Fight for Civil Liberties in the Age of Terror* (New York: Harper Collins, 2008).

Rosenberg, Gerald R. *The Hollow Hope: Can Courts Bring about Social Change?* (Chicago, IL: University of Chicago Press, 2nd edition, 2008).

Rudenstine, David. *The Day the Presses Stopped: A History of the Pentagon Papers Case* (Berkeley, CA: University of California Press, 1998).

Scarry, Elaine. Resolving to Resist (2004) (*Boston Review*, February 1, 2004).

Schauer, Frederick. Categories and the First Amendment: A Play in Three Acts (1981) 34(2) *Vanderbilt Law Review* 265.

Seifter, Miriam. Countermajoritarian Legislatures (2021) 121(6) *Columbia Law Review*.

Seo, Sarah A. *Policing the Open Road: How Cars Transformed American Freedom* (Cambridge, MA: Harvard University Press, 2019).

Sklansky, David. The Fourth Amendment and Common Law (2000) 100 *Columbia Law Review* 1739.

Slobogin, Christopher. *Advanced Introduction to US Criminal Procedure* (Cheltenham, UK: Edward Elgar, 2020).

Stone, Geoffrey. *Perilous Times: Free Speech in Wartime from the Sedition Act of 1798 to the War on Terrorism* (New York: W.W. Norton, 2004).

Strossen, Nadine. *Defending Pornography: Free Speech, Sex, and the Fight for Women's Rights* (New York: Scribner, 1995).

Strossen, Nadine. *HATE: Why We Should Resist it With Free Speech, Not Censorship* (New York: Oxford University Press, 2018).

Strum, Philippa. *When the Nazis Came to Skokie: Freedom for the Speech We Hate* (Lawrence, KA: University Press of Kansas, 1999).

Tomkovicz, James J. *The Right to Assistance of Counsel* (Westport, CT: Praeger, 2002).

Tushnet, Mark. *An Advanced Introduction to Freedom of Expression* (Cheltenham, UK: Edward Elgar, 2018).

Walker, Samuel. *Hate Speech: The History of an American Controversy* (Lincoln, NE: University of Nebraska Press, 1994).

Walker, Samuel. *In Defense of American Liberties: A History of the ACLU* (Carbondale, IL: Southern Illinois University Press, 2nd edition, 1999).

Wermiel, Stephen. 'Magna Carta in Supreme Court Jurisprudence,' in Daniel Magraw et al (eds), *Magna Carta and the Rule of Law* (Chicago, IL: ABA, 2014).

Wheeler, Leigh Ann. *How Sex Became a Civil Liberty* (New York: Oxford University Press, 2014).

Index

Titles in the **Elgar Advanced Introductions** series include:

International Political Economy
Benjamin J. Cohen

The Austrian School of Economics
Randall G. Holcombe

Cultural Economics
Ruth Towse

Law and Development
*Michael J. Trebilcock and Mariana
Mota Prado*

International Humanitarian Law
Robert Kolb

International Trade Law
Michael J. Trebilcock

Post Keynesian Economics
J.E. King

International Intellectual Property
Susy Frankel and Daniel J. Gervais

Public Management and
Administration
Christopher Pollitt

Organised Crime
Leslie Holmes

Nationalism
Liah Greenfeld

Social Policy
Daniel Béland and Rianne Mahon

Globalisation
Jonathan Michie

Entrepreneurial Finance
Hans Landström

International Conflict and Security
Law
Nigel D. White

Comparative Constitutional Law
Mark Tushnet

International Human Rights Law
Dinah L. Shelton

Entrepreneurship
Robert D. Hisrich

International Tax Law
Reuven S. Avi-Yonah

Public Policy
B. Guy Peters

The Law of International
Organizations
Jan Klabbers

International Environmental Law
Ellen Hey

International Sales Law
Clayton P. Gillette

Corporate Venturing
Robert D. Hisrich

Public Choice
Randall G. Holcombe

Private Law
Jan M. Smits

Consumer Behavior Analysis
Gordon Foxall

Behavioral Economics
John F. Tomer

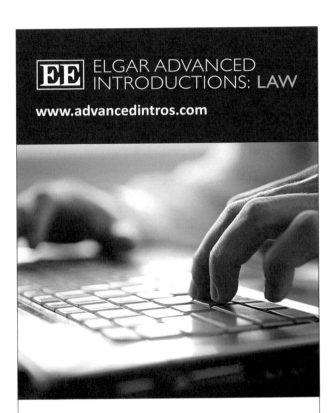